America Reconstituted

Revamping the U.S. Constitution After a 250-year Trial Run

America Reconstituted

Revamping the U.S. Constitution After a 250-year Trial Run

Gary Bergquist

America Reconstituted

Revamping the U.S. Constitution After a 250-year Trial Run

Gary Bergquist

For information address:

Zark Incorporated
23 Ketchbrook Lane
Ellington, CT 06029

ISBN 978-0-9619067-3-3

This book was published by Zark Incorporated

Cover art by Barbara Scavotto-Earley
Artist Rendering by Kevin Kingsley
Printed in the United States of America

10 9 8 7 6 5 4 3 2 1

Dedicated to those with the courage to pull back the curtain.

Table of Contents

Author's Note

Those who have been kind enough to review all or some portions of this book have expressed a common concern: "You'll never get people to agree with such changes to the Constitution. The ideas are too unusual and will never be ratified." Their assumption seems to be that my aim in writing the book is to convince the citizens of the United States to replace the existing Constitution with the one I'm proposing here. If that were the case, my approach would be drastically different. I would need to consider the interests of all parties invested in the result, and I would need to compromise, much as the delegates of the Constitutional Convention did in 1787. However, it's my belief that those compromises have introduced some of the biggest holes in the Constitution. The aim of this book is to fill those holes without being limited by the constraint of compromise.

In other words, I have pursued this endeavor as a work of art, not as a piece of technical writing designed to satisfy the objectives and inhibitions of others. As someone might ask the fanciful question, "What would you do with the money if you won the lottery?", I imagine that someone has asked, "If you could instantly replace the existing Constitution with a new one, what would it look like?" I have freed myself from the impossible requirement that the document must please everyone so that it can be sold to them. Instead, it simply must make sense to me.

What gives me the power to make these decisions, you may be wondering? Nothing, really. You, too, are privileged to live in a free country, so you can do the same. I encourage it.

The experience is enlightening, especially if you share your thoughts with others and welcome their feedback.

Many of my friends, family, and associates have helped to clarify my thinking and my writing. Consequently, the thoughts and propositions on these pages are hardly mine alone. Because of this, I have chosen to use the first-person plural throughout the book ("We propose ...") rather than the first-person singular ("I propose ..."). You should blame me alone, however, for any concepts or wording that are flawed, weak-minded, or just plain offensive. That's on me, and not on those who offered me their time and advice.

Preface

The objective of this book is simple but audacious: revamp the U.S. Constitution.

It's simple because the Constitution is relatively short and direct. The process of revamping should be short and direct as well. Hopefully.

It's audacious because an argument can be made that if it ain't broken, don't fix it. Since the Constitution has held its own for more than two centuries, with a few amendments here and there, it must be doing something right. As a product of the wisest minds in the Colonies, the Constitution has underpinned the world's most successful experiment in democratic representation. Might slight changes to this carefully crafted document be catastrophic?

The question is reasonable. But you can't deny that the long-since-dead men who wrote the Constitution lived in a world we wouldn't recognize. They didn't have electricity. Their idea of unwinding was letting out their girdles and reading a book by candlelight. They lived without the Internet, television, internal combustion engines, movies, airplanes, and light bulbs. Moreover, the participants of the 1787 Constitutional Convention were exclusively white men. The rest of the population had to claw their way into the fabric of the Constitution by way of hard-earned amendments.

We don't doubt that these men were intelligent and courageous trailblazers. It's a wonder that the words coming from their time are still so appropriate to our lives. Nevertheless, it can't hurt to step into their buckled shoes and imagine how one might write the Constitution for our world, not theirs. Having built an amendment process into the Constitution, it's clear they understood that change was inevitable. On one wall of the Jefferson Memorial in Washington D.C. you can find this quote by Jefferson: "I am not an advocate for frequent changes in laws and constitutions. But laws and institutions must go hand in hand with the progress of the human mind. As that becomes more developed, more enlightened, as new discoveries are made, new truths discovered and manners and opinions change, with the change of circumstances, institutions must advance also to keep pace with the times. We might as well requite a man to wear still the coat which fitted him when a boy as civilized society to remain ever under the regimen of their barbarous ancestors."

Our world has undergone much change. Let's follow in the footsteps of our ancestors and have the courage to blaze our own trails. With the advantage of centuries of experience under our belts, let's take a breath and think this through. Our efforts may be good for another few centuries.

Before we get started, though, I need to ask you, dear Reader, for your cooperation. To succeed in this mini-Constitutional Convention, we need to establish some ground rules.

First, let's get our reference points straight. We refer to the U.S. Constitution and its Amendments as the *original* Constitution. You can find it in Appendix A at the back of this book. Since some sentences in the Constitution have been made obsolete or have been revised by Amendments, it seems reasonable to incorporate those Amendments directly into the body of the Constitution. In this way, you won't have to go back and forth between the Constitution and its Amendments to see which words still apply and which have been amended. We refer to this revised Constitution as the *current* Constitution, which can be found in Appendix B. Admittedly, we've taken some liberties in preparing the *current* Constitution, trying to imagine how it would have been written in 1787 if the goals of the 27 Amendments were known and incorporated at the time. Since the purpose of this book is to update the *current* Constitution, which is our logical starting point, we refer to the proposed document as the *new* Constitution. You can find it in Appendix C. You won't be reprimanded for looking at it now; we're not keeping it secret. Since both *current* and *new* Constitutions are organized by the same Articles and Sections, we've placed the two Constitutions side-by-side to make it easier for you to compare them and to see the changes, which are in **bold**.

Second, our aim is not to rewrite every word of the Constitution. Some phrases are too perfect to touch. Our intent is to improve what has not aged well. In the case of antiquated language, we'll suggest plain English, so the document is easier for the modern-day layman to understand.

Third, please note that the first seven words of both Constitutions are the same. These words are the most important words in either Constitution: **We the People of the United States**. We're not just saying this to choke you up and make you feel patriotic. It's the truth and it's important to keep in mind as we rework the Constitution. In the last sentence of Lincoln's Gettysburg Address, he embedded the phrase "government of the people, by the people, for the people." At the risk of seeming overly cynical, the phrase these days might be more accurately stated as "government of the politicians, by the lobbyists, for the corporations." **We the People** sometimes takes a backseat to other forces controlling the direction of our country. To get this new Constitution right, we need to have a single-minded focus on **We the People**. We're asking you to honor your patriotic ancestors by reclaiming and reasserting your personal role in this process. You are more than a pawn.

Fourth, it's naïve to believe the changes being proposed here will be warmly accepted by all. While the changes suggested may benefit **We the People** in general, they may not benefit some people, especially those who have learned to operate within the letter of the law while side-stepping its intent. Expect some resistance.

Fifth, see this book for what it is, an act of revolution. As such, you may want to read it in the privacy of your own bedroom. You don't want to be flagged as a revolutionary, even though you're reading this book. At the heart of any meaningful change is revolution. The American Declaration of Independence begins, "When in the course of human events ..." to invoke a sense of revolt, a sense that the cogs in the machinery of society have reached their limits and shall suffer no more abuse. People shall rise to demand change that acknowledges that there is no machinery without the cogs.

This book hopes to re-instill in you the spirit of revolution. The government of the United States, defined by the U.S. Constitution and founded on the principles of freedom and equal opportunity for all, should work from the bottom up, not from the top down. Power ultimately lies with us. Our strength is the opportunity and responsibility to vote. The power of politicians, lobbyists, corporations, and the rich is the power we grant them. This power is an illusion that fades when the people's collective voice is heard.

Free At Last

Put yourself in the shoes of those drafting the U.S. Constitution at the Constitutional Convention of 1787. After living your life under the oppressive rule of England's King George, you and your countrymen have fought and sacrificed to be allowed control of your destinies. Free at last! Possessing the liberty for which you fought, what do you do with it? Looking back in history, you see that nations have been ruled by kings, emperors, generals, and czars. In no instance were the subjects of these despots free. Leaders have always made the rules. Those living under the rules have fallen in line or been punished. Is it possible to organize a country of free citizens? Will the effort be an attempt at herding cats? How do you keep a group of aspiring despots from coming to power? Will the grand experiment work?

We take for granted the concept of individual freedom. When asked if we are free, most American citizens say yes. If asked what it means to be free, we might say, "I can do what I want to do, how I want to do it, where I want to do it, when I want to do it, and with whom I want to do it." But is this true? What happens if your freedom conflicts with someone else's?

Let's take an example. Suppose two of you are sitting at the dinner table. A box of pizza lies open before you. One slice remains. You both eye it greedily. If you are both truly free, then each of you will be free to do what you want, namely, grab the last slice and eat it. But there's only one slice. As such, the slice of pizza becomes a microcosm of the dilemma of conflicting freedom. There are six possible outcomes.

1. Consideration. One of you remembers the lessons from your parents, that you should consider how other people feel and you should offer to do what will make them happy. You tell the other guy to go ahead and eat the last slice.
2. Tolerance. While you're thinking about whether to take the last slice, the other guy grabs it and starts eating it. You remember the lessons from your parents that not all people are considerate. It's your duty to tolerate their shortcomings. You let the other guy eat the last slice.
3. Compromise. You catch the look in the other guy's eyes. Before he makes a move for the slice, you say, "Split it?" He agrees, and you get out a knife. Each of you gets half a slice.
4. Force. Being bigger and stronger than the other guy, you wrestle him to the floor and sit on his chest as you eat the last slice.
5. Defer to a higher authority. If the higher authority is your mother, you call, "Mom, there's just one slice of pizza left. Who gets it?" Mom's favorite gets the slice.
6. King Solomon. Solomon's solution to the women quarrelling over the baby was to cut the baby in half. By extension, you might surmise that faced with the pizza dilemma the King would cut the pizza in half. If so, you missed the point of the King Solomon parable. Babies don't do as well as pizzas when cut in half. Solomon's solution is that neither of you get the pizza. He'd toss it in the trash or at least move to do so.

This pizza scenario extends to most conflicts of freedom. Let's look at another example. Suppose you're on a flight home from a business trip. It's late in the day and you're exhausted, as are most of the other passengers. You sit down on your seat in the coach section and notice that you have one inch between your knees and the seat in front of you. Each seat has a button that allows the seat to recline one inch.

If you understood the pizza analogy, then you're probably way ahead on this one. As an American, you're free. This means you can do what you want. For example, you can recline your seat to make yourself a bit more comfortable at the expense of the knees behind you. Sadly for you, the passenger in front of you can celebrate the same freedom. We bring up this example because it's likely that you've heard of conflicts arising on airplanes over this seat-reclining freedom. You may have even seen online videos of ensuing altercations.

But let's return to you, in your seat, with this book in your hand, having just read about pizza slices. You size up the situation quickly, knowing there are only six outcomes to this freedom dilemma. First is *consideration*. There may as well be a sticker on the seat recliner button that reads "Inconsiderate." Sure, you're free to push the button and move your seat back so you can be a tad more comfortable, but that decision fails to consider the comfort of your neighbor. Second is *tolerance*. When the person in front of you moves his seat back, you can kick his seat, slap him on the head, and call him a jerk. But a tolerant response would be to grin and bear it. Third is *compromise*. Maybe you move your seat back just half an inch and ask the guy in front of you to do the same. Fourth is *force*. You use your brute force to get your way, and risk being put on TSA's no-fly list. Fifth is *higher authority*. You ask the flight attendant to get involved and let him or her resolve the matter. Sixth is *King Solomon*. The flight attendant heads to the front of the plane to ask the pilot to return to the departure airport so you and your neighbor can be removed from the plane.

What does all of this have to do with the Constitution? Our daily lives have a lot more to do with pizza and airline seats than they do with words in a crumbling old document. Before reworking the Constitution, let's use the pizza scenario to help us understand the dilemma of conflicting freedom. Since freedoms can overlap, problems arise. We need a way to resolve these issues. As we've seen above, there are six ways to handle such conflicts: consideration, tolerance, compromise, force, higher authority, and King Solomon. From this point on, we'll use the word civility to refer to the first three approaches. After all, what are the traits of consideration, tolerance, and compromise but the embodiment of civility, as passed down from our fore-bearers?

The fourth action, force, is the opposite of civility. It's the law of the jungle, the action of the bully.

The fifth action, higher authority, and the sixth action, King Solomon, are our lead-ins to the Constitution and to laws. But before we get there, let's linger on civility. We speak into a void if we justify the need for our Constitution without making clear that laws are a poor but necessary substitute for civility. In a culture of freedom, civility is always an option. You don't need to be civil to others, and others don't need to be civil to you. But it all works better when we're civil to one another. Civility greases the gears of social discourse.

Still, we're human, which means we're flawed. When

we've exhausted our limits of civility and pleasantry fades, we seek rules of a higher authority to guide us. Even with abundant colonial civility, resorting to a higher authority was a bitter, but necessary, pill for the freedom fighters of 1776 to swallow. They had little desire to replace the authority of King George or King Solomon with another. Better to control their own lives and make their own rules. But this meant finding a way that gives everyone an equal voice on what those rules would be.

Laws From Equal Voices

The founding fathers understood the need for rules to resolve conflicts that civility alone cannot resolve. These rules are called *laws*. A law is basically a rule with an associated punishment for not obeying the rule. For example, a law might say that you may not murder someone, and if you do, you're put in prison for life. Or a law might say that when driving a car you must stop at red lights, and if you don't, you pay a $50 fine. A law might say if you rob a bank, you go to jail for fifteen years.

The important thing to note about laws is that, without exception, they curtail freedom. You are not free to murder someone; you are not free to run a red light; and you are not free to rob a bank. As modern-day citizens of America, we don't think of murder and bank-robbing as freedoms lost. But they are, and that fact underscores the fallacy that we are completely free. We cannot do anything we want. Nor do we want our neighbors to do anything they want – not if it interferes with our freedom.

Some laws don't appear to curtail freedom. For example, a law that establishes a national park doesn't seem to hurt anyone. However, the land will be confiscated from those who own it; the resources of the land will be withheld from those who could make a claim to financially exploit it; and the U.S. citizens will pay for the development and maintenance of the park through their taxes. The point is not that laws for establishing national parks should not be passed, but that laws generally curtail freedom in some way.

If we accept the premise that we are free, which we do, then laws have no power to grant rights or freedoms. That would be redundant, since we already possess total freedom. Rather, laws can only remove or restrict our freedom, presumably doing so for the greater good.

The need for laws to govern us begs the question: who shall make and enforce the laws? And thus we arrive at the need for the Constitution: to lay out a framework whereby laws, which abridge freedom, are made and enforced in a land where people view themselves as free. Since laws are rules and consequences that apply to everyone, it makes sense that everyone should have some say in what these laws are.

The second paragraph of the Declaration of Independence reflects the sentiment that we should all have a voice: "We hold these truths to be self-evident, that all men are created equal." We need to exercise some tolerance for Jefferson when reading the words, *all men are created equal.* Today, we see *men* and think *humankind.* In 1776, the word *men* pretty much meant only white landowning men. The sentiment has evolved to mean that all adult citizens in a free nation deserve to be treated the same.

It was this view that led Jefferson to use the clever literary device, *created equal.* However, life's lessons teach us that the opposite is more accurate – we are all unequal, as different as snowflakes. The point that Jefferson was making though, and that we make now, is not that we're all created the same, but rather that we all should have an *equal claim* on our nation's resources and opportunities. Though different from one another, and unequal in physical terms, our equal claim of freedom gives each of us an equal voice.

From the equal-voice principle, it's natural to establish a constitutional framework based on a system of simple voting. Given a decision to be made, each person casts a single vote. Tally the votes. The majority rules. This principle of voting can be applied directly, in which case people vote for or against a proposal, or it can be applied indirectly, in which case people vote for representatives, who in turn vote for or against proposals. A system that uses direct voting is called democracy; a system that votes through elected representatives is called a republic. Our government, as established by the U.S. Constitution, is a representative republic.

The notion that voting is a fair way to make decisions is engrained in our minds. What could be fairer and produce more generally accepted results than a simple vote? If a building is to be painted red or blue, and 101 people get to vote on the color, what method could possibly produce a better result than a simple vote? Whichever color gets 51 or more votes is the winner.

Unfortunately, the one-person-one-vote approach is flawed precisely because of its simplicity. The importance of this issue requires us to take a brief detour to explain the flaw and to suggest an alternative. Let's look at some examples.

Suppose the parents of a family of seven decide to dine out. The parents present two restaurants as alternatives and conduct a vote to determine where they'll go. Each of the seven family members gets one vote. The restaurant with at least four votes is the winner. Seems fair, right? Suppose the restaurants are Adam's Atomic Wings and Bubby's Burgers. With four votes for AAW and three for BB, the family heads off to AAW. Unfortunately, the three members who voted for BB go without food that night because their tongues cannot tolerate the heat of

AAW's food. Still, four are happy, so this is a good outcome, right?

Well, it turns out that everyone in the family enjoys BB's food and would have been happy there. Four of the voters just had a slight preference for heat that night. The problem with the one-person-one-vote method is that it presumes a black and white world. Assuming you love one restaurant and hate the other, you vote for the one you love, and you vote against the one you hate. Whichever side gets more "loves" is the winner. Unfortunately, we don't live in a black and white world. You may love both options, hate both options, or find yourself somewhere in between.

Let's look at the family restaurant vote in two ways, first as a simple vote and second as a vote that more fully reflects the feelings of the voters. Here's the simple vote:

	F1	F2	F3	F4	F5	F6	F7	Total
AAW	X			X		X	X	4
BB		X	X		X			3

The columns represent the seven family members. The rows represent the two restaurants. "X" represents the votes. In this case, AAW wins, four votes to three.

Now suppose each family member expresses their feelings about the restaurants by describing them as Great (3), Good (2), Fair (1), or Poor (0). In other words, they rate the options as if they were restaurant critics, giving each restaurant zero to three stars. Here's the *three-star* vote:

	F1	F2	F3	F4	F5	F6	F7	Total
AAW	3	0	1	3	0	3	3	13
BB	2	3	3	0	3	2	3	16

The first family member (F1) gives AAW three stars and BB two stars. The second family member (F2) gives AAW zero stars because he despises hot food and gives BB three stars. Note that F7 gives both restaurants three stars. When doing the simple vote, he was indifferent but was forced to choose. He flipped a coin, which happened to come up AAW. The Total column shows the sum of the stars. BB wins, sixteen stars to thirteen.

Compare this table of rates (0 to 3) to the previous table of X's. This table better allows you to see how the voters feel and to understand why BB is the better choice in this instance.

You may feel that this method is unfair to those who like hot food. How will they ever get to AAW if they're always out-voted by those who hate hot food? Shouldn't the hot food haters just suck up their misfortune and go without food occasionally? Perhaps, but let's try to lean back on the lessons of civility discussed earlier. The point of voting and of everyone having an equal voice is not that everyone gets their way, but that we strive for the greatest degree of overall satisfaction. This aim is thwarted if you only cast a Yes/No vote and are unable to rate the choices.

In a discussion of voting, it would be unfair not to mention Ranked Choice Voting (RCV), which has gained some popularity in recent years. States that use RCV include Alaska and

Maine. Cities include New York City, San Francisco, and Minneapolis. The idea behind RCV is that you *rank* your choices. Your top preference gets rank 1, your second preference gets rank 2, and so on if there are more than two choices. Here's how the family's restaurant votes look if using RCV:

	F1	F2	F3	F4	F5	F6	F7	Total
AAW	1	2	2	1	2	1	1	4
BB	2	1	1	2	1	2	2	3

AAW has four 1st-place votes and so is the winner, which is the same result as for the simple vote. That's because RCV is meaningful only when there are more than two choices. For example, if the family needed to choose from three restaurants instead of two, then you can meaningfully employ RCV. To illustrate, let's add Paul's Pizza to the list. The votes might look like this:

	F1	F2	F3	F4	F5	F6	F7	Total
AAW	1	3	3	2	3	1	1	3
BB	2	1	1	3	1	3	2	3
PP	3	2	2	1	2	2	3	1

In this case, none of the restaurants have gotten a majority of first-place votes (4 of 7). To resolve this, the RCV method discards the choice with the fewest first-place votes, namely PP, i.e. the third row in the above table. Then, the remaining ranks are adjusted to be just 1s and 2s since there are only two restaurants left. You end up with this:

	F1	F2	F3	F4	F5	F6	F7	Total
AAW	1	2	2	1	2	1	1	4
BB	2	1	1	2	1	2	2	3

which is the same tally as when these were the only two choices. AAW again wins. The only valuable feature of RCV is that you don't have to vote again after eliminating PP. You can just use your pencil and eraser to adjust the ranks. RCV suffers from the same flaw as the one-person-one-vote method – you don't get to express how much you like or dislike the choices. You only get to *rank* your choices, not *rate* them. For this reason, we do *not* recommend RCV.

Suppose Three-Star Voting (TSV) is instead used to *rate* (not *rank*) the three restaurants. The ratings might look like this:

	F1	F2	F3	F4	F5	F6	F7	Total
AAW	3	0	1	3	0	3	3	13
BB	2	3	3	0	3	2	3	16
PP	2	2	2	3	2	2	2	15

which is completely consistent with the RCV vote for each family member but produces an entirely different result, placing AAW last (smallest total) instead of first. By rating instead of ranking, you can clearly "see" how the voters feel about their choices and why the BB restaurant is the best bet tonight.

This discussion applies not only to restaurants but to political candidates. Suppose you're given a choice of four candidates. As you consider each candidate, you may decide you like one and hate the rest. Or you may love two of them and despise the other two. Anything is possible. However, the current one-person-one-vote system forces you to pick exactly one candidate. Your assessment of the other candidates is not solicited. Consequently, you may find yourself engaged in the perverse act of choosing a candidate you don't prefer but consider a more likely winner, or the lesser of two evils. Given four choices, why not be allowed to say what you feel about each one, giving them, say, respective ratings of 3, 3, 1, and 0 stars? If we all have the freedom to rate the candidates as we see fit, the winner is simply the one who gets the most stars. Voters who believe in the pick-one convention still have the freedom to vote for a single candidate, giving him or her 3 stars and 0 stars to the others.

Earlier, we presented a decision by 101 voters of whether to paint a building red or blue, and posed the question, what method could possibly produce a better result than a simple vote? The answer is Three-Star Voting. Instead of voting "Red" or "Blue," each voter rates Red zero to three stars and rates Blue zero to three stars. Whichever color gets the most stars is the winner, and results in a building that will likely be the most generally pleasing to the voters.

Given the need for laws, and given the goal that each member of a free nation has an equal voice in making those laws, it's essential that all voices be heard clearly. A voice is gagged when not allowed to express its full opinion. For example, we sometimes have Presidential elections in which a third-party candidate has significant popularity. In the 1992 election (Bill Clinton, George H.W. Bush, and Ross Perot) and the 2000 election (George W. Bush, Al Gore, and Ralph Nader), the winning candidate got less than 50% of the vote, as the third-party candidate drew away significant voters from the major-party candidates. In both cases, the draw was lopsided, Perot pulling more votes from G.H.W. Bush than from Clinton in 1992, and Nader pulling more votes from Gore than from G.W. Bush in 2000. If the elections had been run using TSV, the likely winner would have been different, being the candidate who the voters would have chosen had the third-party candidate never run. In essence, the traditional voting method punished voters for having two favorites instead of one, allowing the underdog to win.

Let's present one more example to make this crystal clear. Suppose there are three candidates, Bob, Jane, and John. Jane and John are twins and are each loved by 60% of voters. These voters would be happy with either Jane or John as the winner. Bob is loved by the other 40% but disliked by those who love Jane and John. Using the traditional one-person-one-vote method, Bob will win since he will get 40% of the vote while Jane and John each get 30% of the vote as their fans are forced to arbitrarily pick one or the other. Bob, the winner, makes 40% of the electorate happy, while Jane or John would have made 60% happy. This result is not optimal. Using TSV, Jane or John would be the winner as 60% of the voters would give *each* of them three stars while only 40% of the voters would give Bob three stars. Naturally, Jane and John would be unlikely to get *precisely* the same number of votes, so only one would win, or a tie would be broken by coin toss.

One could object to the TSV method on the grounds that it's more complicated than the current pick-one method and may confuse voters. Any benefit from allowing voters to more completely express their feelings about candidates could be lost from mistaken voting brought on by confusion. To assess the validity of this argument, we should look at sample ballots to see if they do appear confusing to the voter.

Here's the current Pick-One ballot, with instructions to pick a candidate by filling in a single circle:

Party	Candidate	Choose
Democrat	Amos	o
Republican	Betty	o
Independent	Curt	x
Green	David	o
Freedom	Betty	o

In this ballot, Curt was selected. Note that candidate Betty appears twice in the ballot because she's been endorsed by two parties. This practice, which is currently permitted in some states, is called fusion voting and gives the candidate the advantage of additional visibility over her opponents.

Here's a Ranked-Choice Voting (RCV) ballot, with instructions to rank the candidates by filling in no more than one circle in each row and column:

Candidate	1st	2nd	3rd	4th
Amos	o	x	o	o
Betty	o	o	o	x
Curt	x	o	o	o
David	o	o	x	o

In this ballot, the voter ranked the candidates Curt, Amos, David, Betty, from first to last.

Here's a Three-Star Voting (TSV) ballot, with instructions to rate the candidates by filling in at most one circle per row:

Candidate	Great(3)	Good(2)	Fair(1)	Poor(0)
Amos	x	o	o	o
Betty	o	o	o	x
Curt	x	o	o	o
David	o	o	x	o

In this ballot, Amos and Curt were rated Great, David Fair, and Betty Poor.

We must concede that filling in one circle is simpler than filling in one circle per candidate, as RCV and TSV require. Some Americans may not be up to the task, so some training may be required. However, the strength of America lies in a tradition of choosing education over settling for the status quo.

Thus, the philosophy of this new Constitution is to use *Three-Star Voting* when it allows a more representative result. *Yes-No Voting*, however, still has its place. If a proposal being addressed is truly a yes/no, black/white, true/false decision, with no shades of grey, then the Yeas or Nays have it. For example, the decision to override a Presidential veto is based on a Yes-No vote that requires two-thirds Yes's. No rating is needed.

Rights

In a nation of free citizens, we begin with the premise that each of us is free to do as we please. However, as stated previously, the possibility of conflicting freedoms forces us to acknowledge the need for laws to restrict those freedoms. The discussion of freedom and laws cannot be complete without considering rights. Since we're proposing a revision to the U.S. Constitution, we must address how the Bill of Rights factors into our claim of freedom and our recognition of the need for laws. In this chapter, we discuss the rationale for these rights, propose some wording changes, and suggest where these rights, introduced in Amendments, properly belong in the new Constitution.

Let's begin by considering how the word *right* is used in our lives: You have the *right* to keep your door closed. She has the *right* to date whomever she wants. I have the *right* to smoke wherever I choose. We have the *right* to breathe clean air. A fetus has the *right* to be born. A woman has the *right* to do with her body as she chooses. I have the *right* to wear what I want. You have the *right* to apply for any job you want. We have the *right* to expect that the food we eat is safe. She has the *right* to have her ears pierced. I have the *right* not to mow my lawn. I have the *right* not to look at un-mowed lawns in my neighborhood.

You can see that the word *right* often comes with emotional baggage. These statements sound more like hopeful pleas than legitimate pronouncements. From this usage, you might infer that a *right* is a claim of freedom to act in some manner.

And sure enough, the definition of a *right* is an *entitlement*. But rights are often claimed without justification for the entitlement.

The word *right* is also used in conjunction with the word *grant*. Those in positions of authority may have the power to grant certain entitlements. For example, a teacher may grant her students the right to use the textbook during an exam. A prison warden may grant a prisoner the right to have visitors on Wednesdays. A king may grant a serf the right to farm on royal property. A slaveowner may grant a slave the right to an extra helping of gruel.

From the Constitutional perspective, neither of these interpretations of the word *right* apply. The Constitution neither entitles us to rights nor does it possess the authority to grant us rights. A document that begins, **We the People**, makes clear that there is no higher authority than the people. The Constitution has no power to grant entitlements to those who empowered it. Rather, since the purpose of the Constitution is to define the framework whereby laws are created that selectively abridge freedom, the word *right* narrowly refers to *guaranteed freedoms*. Certain inherent freedoms must be guaranteed to protect the self-evident power of **We the People**. The history of humankind suggests that civilizations tend toward tyranny. The purpose of Constitutional rights is to **limit the power of the government**, so that **We the People** remain in the driver's seat.

Indeed, the Bill of Rights sets forth these guaranteed freedoms, stating explicitly that Congress shall not pass laws to abridge them: freedom of speech, freedom of religion, freedom of the press, freedom to bear arms, and so on. The question to answer is, why were these freedoms selected, i.e., defined as *rights* in the Bill of Rights? This question is best answered by splitting it into two parts:

1. *Why* did certain freedoms get enshrined as rights in the Constitution?
2. Which freedoms *should* be enshrined as rights?

The answer to the first part requires a look at history. The original Constitution produced by the Constitutional Convention of 1787 did not contain the Bill of Rights. These rights were added four years later as the first ten amendments to the then-ratified Constitution. The Federalists, who pressed for a strong national government, felt there was no need to limit the freedoms that Congress could restrict with laws, since Congress was acting on behalf of the people. If the people jointly wished to abridge certain freedoms, they should be permitted to do so, without limitation. The Anti-Federalists, however, were skeptical of unlimited national power and wanted safeguards in place for certain individual freedoms. Having suffered under the oppression of King George, they sought guarantees. Here's how it played out:

- 11/15/1777 – The Articles of Confederation are adopted by the Continental Congress; these articles treat the colonies as a nation of independent countries.

- 05/25/1787 – The Constitutional Convention convenes to come up with a better arrangement than the Articles of Confederation, which were proving unworkable.

- 09/17/1787 – The Convention concludes with a proposed Constitution, which would become binding once 9 of the 13 states ratified it; it contains no Bill of Rights.

- 12/07/1787 – Delaware is the first state to ratify the Constitution.

- PA, NJ, GA, CT ratify the Constitution in the next few months.

- February 1788 – With further ratification bogged down by the Anti-Federalists, the "Massachusetts Compromise" proposes that a "Bill of Rights" be drawn up as a set of amendments once the Constitution is ratified, since the Constitution cannot be amended until it's ratified.

- Satisfied by this pledge, MA, MD, SC ratify the Constitution in the next few months.

- 06/21/1788 – New Hampshire becomes the ninth of 13 states to ratify the Constitution, which then becomes official.

- 12/15/1788-01/10/1789 – Elections are held to elect federal officials.

- 03/04/1789 – The Federal government begins under the new Constitution.

- James Madison introduces 17 proposed amendments as a "Bill of Rights" per the "Massachusetts Compromise." These amendments are based on existing legal documents, notably the Virginia Declaration of Rights written by George Mason.

- 09/25/1789 – The House and Senate pass 12 of the 17 amendments.

- 05/29/1790 – Rhode Island becomes the final (13th) state to ratify the Constitution.

- 12/15/1791 – The required tenth state finally ratifies 10 of the 12 "Bill of Rights" Amendments, and they become an official part of the Constitution.

This was the timeline by which the Bill of Rights was added to the Constitution. The authors of the Constitution recognized that the ratification process would be stalemated unless a Bill of Rights was included. With the "Massachusetts Compromise" they agreed to do just that. Notice that Madison started with 17 amendments, later pared down by Congress to 12, and further pared down by the state ratification process to ten, which constitutes what we call the Bill of Rights. (Incidentally, the 11th of these proposed amendments was finally ratified in 1992 and became the 27th amendment. It's the amendment that says if Senators or Representatives give themselves a pay raise, it won't take effect until the start of the next Congress. The 12th proposed amendment lays out a scheme for determining the number of Representatives in Congress as the population of the United

States grows. That amendment was never ratified. The number of Representatives has been set at 435 since 1911.)

This timeline answers the first part of our question, *why* these freedoms came to be enshrined. The second part of our question is which freedoms *should* be enshrined.

The Federalists believed the answer was none. They trusted the system as proposed. The Anti-Federalists, however, were uncertain that the government proposed by the Constitution would work as advertised. Looking back on the abuses in the King George era and further back through the endless tradition of authoritarianism, the Anti-Federalists sought guarantees against laws that suppressed popular dissent. They wanted protection for freedom of speech, press, religion, assembly, and petitioning. The voice of the people, when amplified by these freedoms, deters a government's natural spiral toward tyranny. These freedoms, laid out in Amendment 1, exemplify our definition of Constitutional rights as guaranteed freedoms that empower the people.

Beyond these guarantees, the Anti-Federalists insisted that "the right of the people to keep and bear Arms, shall not be infringed" (Amendment 2), and that "no Soldier shall, in time of peace be quartered in any house" (Amendment 3). While these were understandable requirements in 1787, with fresh memories of abuses by the Redcoats and their King, today such rights would do little to deter the tanks and modern weaponry of a despotic regime. As such, they do nothing to empower the people and have been removed from the new Constitution. Control of weapons and military lodging is left as matters of law, as dictated by time, circumstance, and the will of the people.

Let's look at all the guarantees included in the Bill of

Rights so we can evaluate them and assign them a proper place in the Constitution. We've categorized them, abbreviated them a bit, and included corresponding Amendment numbers after each one. And we've included some other Amendments that also deal with guaranteed rights.

Guarantees of free expression –

- Freedom to establish and exercise religion (1)
- Freedom of speech (1)
- Freedom of the press (1)
- Freedom to assemble peaceably (1)
- Freedom to petition the Government for a redress of grievances (1)

Resistance to the King –

- Freedom to keep and bear arms (2)
- Freedom from Soldiers being quartered in any house without consent of the Owner (3)

Anti-discrimination in voting –

- Voting by citizens may not be denied/abridged on account of race, color, or previous condition of servitude (15).
- Voting by citizens may not be denied/abridged on account of gender (19).
- Voting by citizens may not be denied/abridged by reason of failure to pay poll tax or other tax (24).

- Voting by citizens who are eighteen years of age or older may not be denied/abridged on account of age (26).

Rules and procedures of justice –

- Unreasonable searches and seizures are not permitted (4).
- Issuance of Warrants without probable cause is not permitted (4).
- Deprivation of life/liberty/property without due process is not permitted (5).
- Public confiscation of property without just compensation is not permitted (5).
- States laws may not abridge these rules (14S1).

Rules and procedures of criminal justice –

- Being held to answer for capital/infamous crime without presentment/indictment of a Grand Jury is not permitted (5).
- Double jeopardy of life/limb for the same offence is not permitted (5).
- Compelling a witness to provide testimony against oneself is not permitted (5).
- A speedy and public trial, by an impartial jury of the State and district wherein the crime was committed, and to be informed of the nature and cause of the accusation is required (6).
- Available confrontation with the witnesses against the

accused is required (6).

- A compulsory process for obtaining witnesses in his favor and having the Assistance of Counsel for his defense is required (6).
- Excessive bail is not permitted (8).
- Excessive fines are not permitted (8).
- Cruel and unusual punishments are not permitted (8).

Rules and procedures of civil justice (suits of more than $20) –

- Access to trial by jury is required (7).
- Having facts tried by a jury re-examined in any Court of the United States, other than according to the rules of the common law, is not permitted (7).

Reinforcing the premise that citizens are free –

- All other freedoms not guaranteed in the Constitution are retained by the people unless abridged by law (9).
- Only the powers delegated to the United States by the Constitution may be thereby exercised. All other powers are retained by the people, or by the States, as directed by the people (10).

As you can see, these Amendments are a mixed bag. What they have in common is the guarantee of freedom required to keep power in the hands of the people. Let's discuss these categories one at a time and find a place for them in the new Constitution.

The first category, *Guarantees of free expression*, ensures us the ability to speak our minds and, in so doing, to persuade others to our way of thinking. As currently stated, these rights, if interpreted absolutely, can infringe on the freedom of others. Take for example freedom of speech. In the 1919 U.S. Supreme Court case Schenck v. United States, Justice Oliver Wendell Holmes Jr. expressed the view that freedom of speech was not unlimited if the words created a "clear and present danger," such as falsely shouting "Fire" in a crowded theater. Likewise, slander and libel are examples of free speech being taken too far and requiring legal limitations.

Here's the proposed re-wording of these rights in the new Constitution, which can be found in Section 5 of Article IV:

> *Given that Tyranny suffers at the Voice of Free People and that this Constitution is the embodiment of that Voice, Congress shall make no law abridging freedom of expression that does not cause or incite destruction or injury and is not false and defamatory, such expression including religious exercise, freedom of speech or of the press, assembly of the people, and petitioning the Government for a redress of grievances.*

Note that this wording both broadens and narrows Amendment 1 and provides a leading phrase to justify its intent. The word "*expression*" is used to cover other means of communication that may arise in the future. The words "*does not incite destruction or injury and is not false and defamatory*" are included to keep bad actors from using *free speech* arguments to justify poor behavior. The words "*religious exercise*" replace "*an establishment of religion or ... the free exercise thereof*" so that government involvement in religion is limited to the recognition of religion as an exercise of expression.

The Amendments in the second category, *Resistance to the King*, are removed from the new Constitution, as mentioned above.

The third category, *Anti-discrimination in voting*, includes rights required to fulfill Jefferson's *created equal* claim. Rather than enumerating the historical forms of discrimination, and trying to anticipate future areas of discrimination, let's replace them with a single clause, some of this coming from Section 1 of the 14th Amendment. This clause can be found in the new Constitution under Article IV, Section 2:

> *All persons born or naturalized in the United States, and subject to the jurisdiction thereof, are citizens of the United States and of the State wherein they reside. No State shall make or enforce any law which shall abridge the privileges or immunities of citizens of the United States; nor shall any State deprive any person of life, liberty, or property, without due process of law; nor deny to any person within its jurisdiction the equal protection of the laws. Citizens having attained the age of eighteen years shall be permitted to vote. The right of citizens of the United States to vote in any primary or other election for President or Vice President or Senator or Representative in Congress, shall not be denied or abridged by the United States or by any State by reason of failure to pay any poll tax or other tax, or for any reason except age if under eighteen years.*

The next three categories involve *Rules and procedures*

of justice. As such, they are about guaranteeing that we are treated fairly and with dignity when we are suspected of or charged with going afoul of the law. The thrust of these amendments is important enough to justify the new Section 6 under Article IV of the new Constitution, whose wording is taken directly from Amendments 4, 5, 6, 7, 8, and 14:

> *The right of the people to be secure in their persons, houses, papers, and effects, against unreasonable searches and seizures, shall not be violated, and no Warrants shall issue, but upon probable cause, supported by Oath or affirmation, and particularly describing the place to be searched, and the persons or things to be seized.*

> *No person shall be held to answer for a capital, or otherwise infamous crime, unless on a presentment or indictment of a Grand Jury, except in cases arising in the armed forces, or in the Militia, when in actual service in time of War or public danger; nor shall any person be subject for the same offence to be twice put in jeopardy of life or limb; nor shall be compelled in any criminal case to be a witness against himself, nor be deprived of life, liberty, or property, without due process of law; nor shall private property be taken for public use, without just compensation.*

> *In all criminal prosecutions, the accused shall enjoy the right to a speedy and public trial, by an impartial jury of the State and district wherein the crime shall have been committed, which district shall have been previously ascertained by law, and to be informed of the nature and cause of the accu-*

sation; to be confronted with the witnesses against him; to have compulsory process for obtaining witnesses in his favor, and to have the Assistance of Counsel for his defense.

In Suits at common law, where the value in controversy shall exceed twenty dollars, the right of trial by jury shall be preserved, and no fact tried by a jury, shall be otherwise re-examined in any Court of the United States, than according to the rules of the common law.

Excessive bail shall not be required, nor excessive fines imposed, nor cruel and unusual punishments inflicted.

No State shall make or enforce any law which shall abridge the provisions of this Section.

The final category, Reinforcing the premise that citizens are free, contains the 9th and 10th amendments, each of which makes claims that should be obvious in a nation of free citizens. The 9th amendment claims that if any freedom is not "enumerated" as a right by the Constitution, it nevertheless remains your freedom unless it is curtailed by law. The 10th amendment says that "powers" not delegated to the United States, nor prohibited from the States, by the Constitution remain up for grabs. In other words, the Constitution does not control what it does not claim to control. Though superfluous, these two amendments remain in the new Constitution as Article IV Section 9, to reinforce what may not be obvious to everyone:

The enumeration in the Constitution, of certain rights, shall not be construed to deny or disparage others retained by the people. The powers not delegated to the United States by the Constitution, nor prohibited by it to the States, are reserved to the States respectively, or to the people.

Scope of Law

Each of us is a member of a nation, a state, a county, and a town or city. Since these governing bodies can pass laws, what happens when the laws contradict one another? For example, suppose the Federal Government passes a law prohibiting you from building your home within 50 feet of a river. Suppose your State passes a law prohibiting you from building your home closer than 25 feet. Suppose your Town passes a law prohibiting you from building your home closer than 100 feet. Which jurisdiction wins? How close to the river can you build your home?

Assume that each level of government is controlled by its own Constitution, and that the Constitutions have gone through a reasonable vetting and ratification process. As a citizen or resident of the jurisdiction (Nation, State, Town), you have a voice in making its laws, and you have an obligation to live by those laws. As such, it makes sense that you must abide by the most restrictive law of the three jurisdictions: your home can be no closer than 100 feet of a river. In this way, you abide by the laws of all three jurisdictions.

Can the Federal Government overrule your Town so that 50 feet is acceptable? Can your State overrule the Federal Government so that 25 feet is acceptable? In other words, can one government overrule another one to make the law *less* restrictive? It's natural to think that if one jurisdiction is more powerful than another, then the larger jurisdiction can impose its will on the lesser jurisdiction. Since a Nation is bigger than a State, and since a State is bigger than a Town, the larger entities are generally believed to have the power to overrule the laws of *lesser* entities. This authoritarian wording is apparent in Article VI, Clause 2 of the current Constitution:

> *This Constitution, and the Laws of the United States which shall be made in Pursuance thereof; and all Treaties made, or which shall be made, under the Authority of the United States, shall be the supreme Law of the Land; and the Judges in every State shall be bound thereby, any Thing in the Constitution or Laws of any State to the Contrary notwithstanding.*

This passage has come to be known as the Supremacy Clause, since it states that the U.S. Constitution and the laws derived from it are *the supreme Law of the Land.* In the example above, however, abiding by the Town law (100 feet) does not violate the Federal law (50 feet) or the State law (25 feet). Common sense and respect for the laws of all jurisdictions lead us to infer that the most restrictive of the laws should apply, claims of supremacy notwithstanding. In other words, the Federal law does not need to negate the Town law.

This example is rather simple, though. Instead, suppose laws conflict to such a degree that both cannot be obeyed. For example, let's assume Federal law requires that you cover your house with a metal roof, while State law requires that you use asphalt shingles. In this instance, it's not clear which law is more restrictive, one that requires metal roofs or one that requires asphalt roofs. To resolve the contradictory laws, one can make a case for supremacy of the Federal law: roofs must be made of metal; the State law is invalid. This leads us to conditional supremacy: The most restrictive law of any jurisdiction is the most binding if less restrictive laws of superior jurisdictions are still honored, but in the case of contradiction, laws of the superior jurisdiction prevail. This philosophy is already stated implicitly in the Supremacy Clause via the words, "...any Thing in the Constitution or Laws of any State to the *Contrary notwithstanding*."

Let's consider another example. Suppose Federal law restricts your freedom to have an abortion, disallowing the procedure after five months of pregnancy. Suppose State law restricts your freedom to have an abortion at any time. By the reasoning above, the State law is more restrictive and thus applies to anyone in that State. By obeying the State law, you are also obeying the Federal law. From a legal perspective, both jurisdictions are satisfied. Though one might argue that the Supremacy Clause should apply, adherence to the State law does not conflict with adherence to the Federal law.

To skirt this interpretation, pro-abortion advocates might lobby to pass a Federal law that prohibits states from passing laws that infringe on the freedom to have an abortion before five months. However, the function of laws is to restrict the freedom of its citizens, not to restrict the freedom to pass legislation. Establishing rules and restrictions on legislation is a function of the Constitution, not of the legislature. In other words, pro-abortion advocates would be on sounder legal grounds lobbying for a Constitutional amendment along the lines of, "*The right of the people to have an abortion before five months of pregnancy shall not be infringed.*"

This wording, of course, recalls the second amendment in the Bill of Rights: "... *the right of the people to keep and bear Arms, shall not be infringed.*" Earlier, in our discussion on rights, we removed this wording from the Constitution, making restrictions on the freedom to keep and bear arms a matter of law, not a matter of constitutional rights. The freedom to own a gun is not essential to the constitutional aim of ensuring that the workings of the government shall reflect the will of the people.

Stated simply, the starting point is freedom. We are all free to do what we choose, be it to have a gun or an abortion. Our fellow citizens may decide, through our duly elected representatives, to pass laws that restrict these freedoms to some degree. And the laws may change over time. But these decisions belong to us, through our representatives, and not to the drafters of the Constitution. Should the views of our fellow citizens not conform with our own at any given time, we remain free to leave the jurisdiction so we can reside with like-minded individuals.

While common sense leads us to conclude that Federal restrictions on individual freedom trumps State restrictions on those freedoms, there is no inherent implication that the Federal government has the power to control how we live our lives. Likewise, there is no implication or wording in the Constitution that allows the Federal government to dictate how States should run their jurisdictions. In fact the 10th Amendment pretty much states the opposite:

> *The powers not delegated to the United States by the Constitution, nor prohibited by it to the States, are reserved to the States respectively, or to the people.*

However, in its attempt to make the country a better place, Congress sometimes oversteps its authority by compelling

State agencies to assist with administration of its legislation. Examples of these are the Low-Level Radioactive Waste Policy Amendments Act of 1985 (having States take title to undisposed waste), the Professional and Amateur Sports Protection Act of 1992 (prohibiting sports gambling in some States but not others), and the Brady Handgun Violence Prevention Act of 1993 (requiring State officials to conduct background checks). Flush with the heady goal of solving perceived national problems, members of Congress sometimes write laws that coerce State governments into becoming participants in their legal solutions. Nothing in the Supremacy Clause says they can do this. In each of these three cases, suits made their way to the Supreme Court challenging these laws. In each case, the Supreme Court repealed all or parts of the laws via rulings whose reasoning has become known as the *anti-commandeering doctrine*. Basically, the Federal government cannot commandeer the State jurisdictions to do their bidding. If the goal is noble enough, the Federal government has plenty of agencies and offices to take on the new responsibilities required by a new law.

Arguments have been made that in times of national emergency State resources may need to be commandeered and the Constitution should allow for such commandeering. However, experience has demonstrated that the separate States and the People have always risen to the call. To open the Constitutional door to emergency commandeering will then open the door to conveniently redefining the term *emergency*.

To make these understandings explicit, we have reworded the Supremacy Clause under Article VI:

This Constitution, and the Laws of the United States which shall be made in Pursuance thereof; and all Treaties made, or which shall be made, under the Authority of the United States, shall be the supreme Law of the Land; and the Judges in every State shall be bound thereby, any Thing in the Constitution or Laws of any State to the Contrary notwithstanding.

The powers not delegated to the United States by the Constitution, nor prohibited by it to the States, are reserved to the States respectively, or to the people. Powers thereby exercised by the States shall not be commandeered under Laws of the United States.

Apportionment

Apportionment is the process by which each State is allocated a certain number of members to the House of Representatives.

The Senate comprises 100 Senators, two per State. For matters that come before the Senate, each State has an equal voice. The House of Representatives comprises 435 Representatives, with the Representatives apportioned to the States according to their respective populations. For matters that come before the House, the voice of each State is therefore proportional to its population. The underlying philosophy is that decisions that affect States equally should be the province of the Senate, while decisions that affect people equally should be the province of the House.

Here's a simple way to view the role of Representatives. At present, each House member represents about 780,000 people. Imagine the population of the United States being divided into 435 congressional Districts of that size. You can view them as mini-States. One District might be in the Midwest and be largely populated by people associated with corn farming. Another might be on the Gulf Coast and populated by people heavily involved in oil drilling and refining. Another might consist of city workers in an urban area of a large metropolitan city.

The idea is that each of these Districts contains people whose views and interests have something in common since they're neighbors. The people of the District vote for a single person to represent their common views. That Representative has one vote in the House to give some voice to the people of his or her District. This is the objective of the House.

In practice, this ideal has problems. First, who draws up the Districts? Second, since the people of the United State are mobile, how do we dynamically adjust the Districts so they each contain roughly the same number of people? Third, as States are added to the Union, and as population increases, how many total Representatives should there be, and how exactly should they be apportioned to the states? Fourth, at 780,000 people per District, are the interests of the people homogeneous enough that any Representative can properly represent them?

The existing Constitution is not specific on how to answer these questions. These are the Constitutional directives, as currently amended; *Enumeration* is Constitution-speak for *Census*:

> *Representatives shall be apportioned among the several States according to their respective numbers, counting the whole number of persons in each State, excluding Indians not taxed. ... The actual Enumeration shall be made ... every ... Term of ten Years, in such Manner as [Congress] shall by Law direct ... but each State shall have at least one Representative.*

> (As of the 1940 Census, all Native Americans were counted for apportionment, so the phrase "Indians not taxed" no longer applies.)

Given these broad instructions, it's hard to imagine that the apportionment process would be consistently applied. Indeed, the procedure for apportioning Representatives has varied and evolved considerably, partly because of the Union's growth in terms of both population and States, and partly because of partisan politics at the time of apportionment.

Before the first Census in 1790, the total number of Representatives was set at 65 for the 13 States, with a cap of one Representative per 30,000 citizens. After that, the total number of Representatives changed every 10 years from 1790 to 1911 by various schemes. In 1911, the number was finally fixed at 435, for reasons of efficiency in terms of office space, clerical help, the size of the House Chamber, and the effort required to manage such a large group.

As the number of Representatives evolved, so did the procedure for apportioning House seats to the States. There have been five different methods: Jefferson Method [1790-1830], Webster Method [1840], Vinton/Hamilton Method [1850-1900], Method of Major Fractions [1910, 1930], and Method of Equal Proportions [1940-present].

The methods vary in several ways. Some start with the desired number of people per Representative, while others start with the desired total number of Representatives. When resolving a non-whole number of Representatives for a State, such as 7.63, some methods discard the fractional part, giving the State 7 Reps; some round to the nearest whole number, giving the State 8 Reps; and some do it other ways.

As directed by the Constitution, the Census is conducted every ten years beginning in 1790. At times, politics have gotten in the way of the apportionment process. After the 1920 Census, an apportionment never took place. Representatives from rural districts were concerned over the likelihood of losing seats to urban districts and so claimed the census was inaccurate. They had enough sway in Congress to block reapportionment, the next apportionment taking place after the 1932 election.

Then there's the matter of dividing a State into its Congressional Districts. Congress passes this responsibility on to the States, citing Article 1, Section 4 of the Constitution, which states that "The Times, Places and Manner of holding Elections for Senators and Representatives, shall be prescribed in each State by the Legislature thereof." Though this passage refers only to *holding elections*, it's been broadly interpreted to apply also to defining Districts.

Over time, the States have used three methods for defining Districts to allocate their Representatives:

Single-Member Districts have one Representative per District. The State must be divided into as many Districts as the State has Representatives. How those lines are drawn is up to the respective State Legislatures. In 1842, a requirement was passed that the Districts must be *contiguous*. A contiguous District is one in which you can travel between any two points in the District without passing through another District. In 1872, an additional requirement was passed that the Districts have an approximately *equal number* of inhabitants. In 1901, a further requirement stated that the Districts must be *compact*. A compact District is geographically consolidated and looks more like a clam than an octopus. The aim of these restrictions was to enforce the intent of the Constitution, thereby thwarting the actions of partisan politicians to gerrymander their State's Districts.

Multi-Member Districts are those Districts that have more than one Representative. For example, in the 3rd Congress, Massachusetts had thirteen Representatives spread over four Districts (having 2, 3, 4, and 4 Reps). In a District with four Representatives, the voters of the District get to vote for all four Reps. This type of districting was banned in 1967 by the Uniform Congressional District Act (UCDA).

At-Large Districts are like Multi-Member Districts but taken to the extreme. A State that has At-Large Districts is considered one big Multi-Member District. For example, Connecticut had between five and seven Representatives from 1789 to 1837. During that period, the State was not geographically divided into Districts. Rather, all voters had the opportunity to vote for all Representatives. Some States have had a combination of Single-Member Districts and At-Large Districts. Typically, this occurred when a State was assigned by apportionment an additional Representative or two. Instead of redrawing the Districts, the State simply placed the new Reps in an At-Large District, in which all State voters got to participate. As with Multi-Member Districts, At-Large Districts were banned in 1967 under the UCDA.

Single-Member Districts are the current law per the UCDA. If the aim of the UCDA in 1967 was to enforce the design aims of the Constitution, one would have expected that *contiguous*, *equal number*, and *compact* would have been included as District requirements in the Act. They were not. Though required in earlier legislation, these provisions were omitted from the UCDA. State Legislatures are free to draw District lines any way they choose. Which brings us to gerrymandering.

Gerrymandering is the practice of drawing District lines in such a way that one political party is favored over another. Here's a picture to help you see the clever process:

District	Orange Party	Yellow Party
1	60	40
2	60	40
3	60	40
4	60	40
5	10	90
Total	**250**	**250**

In this fictional State, there are five Districts and a total of 500 residents. Note that the residents are evenly split between the Orange and the Yellow political parties. One might expect the Reps to be also somewhat evenly split between the parties. In this case, the District lines have been drawn in such a way that four of the Districts have 60 Orange residents and 40 Yellow residents, while one District has 10 Orange residents and 90 Yellow residents. In this way, four of the Districts have populations that significantly favor the Orange party, increasing the chances that there will be four Orange Reps to one Yellow Rep.

The essential requirement of gerrymandering is Single-Member Districts. With At-Large Districts there are no lines for the State Legislature to draw so gerrymandering is not possible. During discussions for the UCDA, no legislator was so transparent as to cite gerrymandering as an argument for Single-Member Districts. Instead, the evils of At-Large Districts were argued. A key point was that At-Large voting in southern states would worsen the odds of racial minorities being able to elect minority representatives. We can illustrate their argument by altering the above table just a bit:

District	Majority	Minority
1	65	35
2	65	35
3	65	35
4	65	35
5	15	85
Total	**275**	**225**

In this fictional State, the minority vote has the majority in just a single district. If you switch to At-Large voting, all State voters can weigh in on the five Representatives at a proportion of 275 to 225, possibly causing the minority voters to end up with no Representatives. In short, if you're part of a significant minority, then Single-Member Districts can seem to be a good thing since you get at least some representation out of it.

This argument is specious because of its questionable presumptions:

1. That the voters of this State are strongly racist and consistently rate the skin color of the candidate above other traits.

2. That the minority population of a State so segregated in this fashion, whether by gerrymandering or by happenstance, should be pleased with one Rep out of five even though their population mix, 225 out of 500, would suggest two or three Reps.

3. That a connection exists between race and political party, with the candidates in each District contest being

neatly divided between a minority candidate and a majority candidate, per this assumed party racism.

4. That At-Large voters will consistently vote for the candidates of all Districts according to their party or race preference.

On this last point, we can use history as a guide. Senators are elected using the At-Large method. States are not divided into two Districts, one for each Senator. Rather, voters of each State get to vote for both Senators of their state. If At-Large voting follows the pattern suggested by the fourth presumption above, then one would expect that Senators from most States would belong to the same party, namely the party of the majority population. "Split" Senators (one from each political party) would be rare. In the 91st Congress (1969-1970), the first Congress after the passage of the UCDA, 22 of the 50 States had split Senators, certainly not a rarity.

Given the average House District population of 780,000, it's become difficult to imagine Districts as homogeneous communities of corn farmers or fishermen. The constitutional ideal of Districts being small enough that their single Representative can speak for the group is a fading memory. The act of drawing District lines has become little more than an exercise by State legislatures to promote the voice of their majority parties. Still, the constitutional directive remains that each State shall have a voice in the House proportional to its population. To fulfill this aim and to remove the ability to gerrymander, the new Constitution requires At-Large voting for House members as well as Senators.

Also, since the dream of homogeneity in a District is unattainable, there's no point in having so many Representatives. The country has gone from 65 to 435. As of 2025, California has 52 Reps and Texas has 38. True, the population of these states justifies this many Reps given that there is a total of 435. But what good comes from having this large a House? In the new Constitution, the total number of Reps is reduced to 200. If the Senate can manage with 100, the House can surely manage with 200. As such, California and Texas will have about 23 and 17 Reps respectively. This provides enough Reps to convey the wants and needs of the citizens of these populous States. See Appendix D.

Here is the revised description for apportionment (within Article 1, Section 2), wordier than the original but less prone to misinterpretation or reinterpretation:

Representatives shall be apportioned among the several States which may be included within this Union, according to their respective Numbers, which shall be determined as the whole number of persons in each State.

The actual Enumeration shall be made every Term of ten Years, in the Year whose number is wholly divisible by ten, in such Manner as the Congress of the United States shall by Law direct. The Enumeration shall count each person's State of residence as of the first day of April of the Enumeration Year. The results of the Enumeration shall be reported to the President and the Speaker of the House of Representatives by the 31st day of December of the Enumeration Year. The Clerk of the House shall determine reapportionment and inform each State Governor of the number of its House Representatives by the 25th day of January of the Year following the Enumeration Year. Reapportionment shall be determined by the Method of Equal Proportions:

1. *Let E[i] be the Enumeration for State i and let T be the Total number of seats to be apportioned (200).*
2. *Let N[i] be the Number of seats allocated to State i so far, initially setting N[i] to 1 as the mandated minimum.*
3. *Set R as the number of remaining seats to be apportioned: T minus the sum across N[i].*
4. *Set A[i] as the priority value for State i: E[i] divided by the square root of the product of N[i] and N[i]+1.*
5. *Increment N[i] by 1 seat for the State whose value A[i] is largest. Decrement R by 1.*
6. *Repeat steps 4 and 5 until R is zero. N[i] is the apportionment for State i.*

Admittedly, this wording is someone complex for the layman. Nonetheless, this is the precise method currently used by Congress for apportioning the 435 Reps. The details are included in the Constitution to prevent any alteration for political gain and to allow review by the citizens of the United States.

Here is the revised description for Elections for Senators and Representatives (within Article 1, Section 4):

The Times, Places and Manner of holding Elections for Senators and Representatives, shall be prescribed in each State by the Legislature thereof; but the Congress may at any time by Law make or alter such Regulations. Voting shall be At

Large for Senators and Representatives, with ballots for voters of each State comprising all candidates of that State eligible in that Election. No information about the candidate other than name shall appear on the ballot, and each name shall not be listed more than once. The Three Star Voting method shall be used, in which the voter shall rate each candidate on a three-to-zero scale (3=Excellent, 2=Good, 1=Fair, 0=Poor). The total number shall be tallied by candidate. Candidates with the highest tallies for the available offices shall be elected. Ties shall be resolved by coin-toss of the State Governor.

Inflation

The word *inflation* refers to the condition of an economy in which prices increase over time. The price of any given commodity, such as a gallon of gasoline, a pound of hamburger, or an ounce of gold, normally moves up and down based on the vagaries of supply and demand, sales promotions, and other quirks of the free market. However, during periods of inflation, the average price of a commodity tends to continually trend upward so that pretty much everything we buy costs more. Spending more dollars to buy the same item means the dollar itself is worth less.

The specific causes of inflation are numerous and need not concern us here. The important point is that we live in inflationary times. This was not always the case. In fact, the Unites States did not experience inflation until 1933.

One of the ways to measure inflation is to look at the price of a particular commodity: gold. How many dollars does it take to buy one ounce of gold? In 1787, the official U.S. Government price of an ounce of gold was $19.49. The price of gold changed slightly over the following decades but remained roughly $20 per ounce until 1933, when the U.S. ended the gold standard for domestic transactions. The gold standard was a pledge by the U.S. Government to exchange a fixed amount of gold for a U.S. Dollar. With that guarantee cancelled, the price of gold slowly moved upward to about $40 per ounce by 1971, when the United States ended the gold standard altogether. Since then, the price of gold has continued to increase, as a direct result of the dollar's weakening purchasing power.

The reason this matters to us is that the U.S. Constitution explicitly refers to *dollars*. In the Constitution of 1787, there are two references to dollars. One is in Article II, Section 9:

> *... a Tax or duty may be imposed on such Importation, not exceeding ten dollars for each Person.*

The other is in Amendment VII within the Bill of Rights:

> *In Suits at common law, where the value in controversy shall exceed twenty dollars, the right of trial by jury shall be preserved, ...*

Though the first reference was rendered moot by the 13th Amendment, the second reference still applies. Its intent is to protect our rights to a civil trial if the contested amount is significant, namely twenty dollars, or about one ounce of gold. At the time, the dollar was believed to have an unchanging value. Writing *twenty dollars* had approximately the same effect as writing *one ounce of gold*. The former was used in the Constitution because the dollar was the national currency. However, due to inflation, twenty dollars in 1787 had far greater buying power than twenty dollars does today. At the start of 2025, the market price of gold was $2600 per ounce, or about 130 times what it was in 1787. This means that twenty dollars could buy only 1/130th of an ounce of gold at the start of 2025. To have the same Constitutional effect, namely, to ensure the rights to a civil trial if the contested value is worth more than one ounce of gold, the words *twenty dollars* should instead be *twenty-six hundred dollars* at the start of 2025.

To maintain the intent of these original words, the Constitution would need to be amended frequently with inflated dollar values. Instead of doing that, the phrase *twenty dollars* could be replaced by *the value of one ounce of gold.* Though this proposal would resolve the problem of inflation, it would introduce a degree of instability. After all, the value of an ounce of gold varies by the minute on the gold commodities market. Let's instead propose this phrase: *the value in dollars of one ounce of gold as of the start of the current calendar year.* For example, on the close of December 31st of 2019, the price of gold was $1519.50. On December 31st of 2023, the price was $2062.90. Allowing nominal rounding, let's call the respective values $1520 and $2065. This means the right to a civil trial would be guaranteed for amounts contested in 2020 of $1520 or more, and for amounts contested in 2024 of $2065 or more. You can see that the amount inflates over time but remains constant within any calendar year. Let's coin the word *Goldar* to represent this amount:

> *Goldar: the value in dollars of one ounce of gold as of the start of the current calendar year.*

The justification for specifying value in terms of gold in the Constitution is that history has shown that the value of gold is constant not only across centuries, but across millennia. By *value*, we don't mean its *price*, but rather its *worth*, i.e. what you can trade for it. As an exercise, pick a past date and an item that could be purchased both then and now: a meal, a set of clothes, a house, a farm animal, a wagon, a pair of shoes, a bottle of wine. Use the internet to determine the cost of that item *in gold* then and now. You'll find that the cost remains in the same ballpark. The purchasing power of gold, because of its scarcity, has been relatively stable over the years. The purchasing power of dollars, on the other hand, declines each year due to inflation. The price in dollars of a farm animal or a bottle of wine increases over time.

For a Goldar to serve its function, it must have two seemingly contradictory traits. It must increase over long periods to keep pace with inflation, and it must be unchanged for short periods. The definition above satisfies both requirements. The Goldar is reset once every year, on January 1st. On that day, the Secretary of the Treasury sets the Goldar dollar amount based on the closing value of gold the day before. That static dollar amount remains in effect for twelve months until it is again reset.

It may seem that greater accuracy can be achieved by resetting the Goldar more frequently, say every month. However, accuracy is not the prime motivation here. The point of the Goldar is to provide a unit of currency within the Constitution that is stable and that adjusts itself over time. Applying this new terminology to the second passage above we get,

> *In Suits at common law, where the value in controversy shall exceed one Goldar, the right of trial by jury shall be preserved, ...*

In 1787, one Goldar was $20. In 2022, it was $1520. In 2024, it was $2065. You can see that this scheme works well to implement the architects' intent, which is to avoid jury trial for piddling amounts such as twenty dollars now. Note that the value of a Goldar is taken at the time of the financial transaction, in this case at the time of the "controversy."

If the new Constitution contained only the same two references to dollars as the current Constitution, we likely would not be suggesting the use of Goldars. However, the new Constitution, as you will see, includes more currency references. It makes sense to formally and finally address the inflation problem. Here is the Constitutional definition of a Goldar in Article II, Section 5:

A Goldar is a number of U.S. dollars at a point in time. The exact number shall be set by the Secretary of Treasury of the United States on the 1st day of January of each year, based on the prevailing price of one ounce of gold. The number is effective for that calendar year. Any reference to a Goldar assumes its value as of the date of the applicable financial transaction.

Political Parties

The President presents the State of the Union Address annually, as required under Article II, Section 3 of the Constitution. Gathered in a single room are all the officers designated by the U.S. Constitution: President, Vice President, Senators, Representatives, and Supreme Court Justices. Since the Address is now broadcast live on television and the internet, the American people can listen to the President and watch those who represent us. Viewers who are not familiar with this spectacle might be confused by the dynamics of recent sessions. One has the sense of watching two schools of fish. The first school rises as a unit when the President reaches an applause point. The other remains seated, dismally shaking their heads or shouting insults. The behavior, as we've come to expect, reflects partisan politics. Attendees in the same party as the President rise while those in the opposing party remain seated.

Though belonging to opposing political parties, the attendees have one thing in common: they have sworn allegiance to the Constitution and to the people of the United States as a requirement of their positions. As we observe their partisan antics at this annual Address, we can't help but wonder where their allegiance truly lies – to the parties, or to the people?

Imagine Abraham Lincoln at the lectern looking at our country's leaders with sad eyes and worn countenance, shaking his head. "A nation divided cannot stand," he might again say. Not since the Civil War have the people of the United States been so fraught with discord. Brother against brother. Family against family. The animus of our leaders has leached down to those they represent.

As humans, we find comfort in community, in belonging to something larger than ourselves. On both sides of the partisan divide, we take pride in the United States, a country like no other. However, opinion polls show the approval rating of the three branches of government continue to sink. Yet we willingly march to the polls on election day to vote for those who belong to our political party. Intellectually we know that our leaders are failing us, but emotionally we are so hungry to belong, that we step forward as feeders at their buffet of half-truths.

And half-truths they are. Our leaders exploit thorny issues: immigration, social welfare, abortion, gun control, international relations, and so on. These problems resist simple solutions. The pros and cons of any approach that addresses these issues fairly are weighty enough to demand compromise. But rather than commit to the unpopular process of compromise, our leaders take the position promoted by their party and spin a web of vitriolic half-truths to support it. We recognize half-truths by the fact that neither party attempts to explain why the opposing party might reasonably believe as they do. Instead, positions are sealed by berating those on the other side, claiming or implying that their opponents are ignorant, self-serving, or complicit.

Once We the People accept this deceit, the circle is complete. We offer our loyalty in exchange for partisan promises of what these politicians will do for us as our leaders. Using half-truths for justification, our elected representatives explain that if nothing gets done it's not their fault – it's due to stonewalling by the other party.

The U.S. Constitution makes no mention of political parties. This fact is remarkable when you consider how heavily political parties have influenced our government then and now. In most elections for federal office, two of the candidates come from the two major parties. Sometimes these are the only two candidates. They are selected by a process designed and sanctioned by the parties. The candidates preferred by the heads of the parties and by the major donors are the favorites to find their names on the ballot. In many states, only voters registered in those parties are permitted to vote in the primary elections.

With so much power being wielded by political parties, it seems appropriate for the Constitution to either formalize their role or to set rules that restrict that power. The founding principle of the Constitution is that all power flows from **We the People**. The guiding principle of political parties is that the selection of candidates, and hence power, flows from *We the Parties*. Favoring the Constitution, we propose taking power from the parties and returning it to the people.

To address how this can be done within the Constitution, we first need to understand the source of power. The Democratic and Republican parties, currently the two most influential parties, are massive political organizations funded by wealthy donors and staffed by loyal party members. In theory, each party maintains a *platform* of positions, which are presumably beneficial to the country if enacted. Those who agree with the platform are encouraged to join the party and to support it with their money, their activity, and their votes. Loyal party members typically vote along party lines, picking candidates based on the party to which they belong. The party organization, meanwhile, invests its formidable resources in finding and grooming candidates that the party leaders believe will toe the party line. The selected candidates get the financial and promotional support they require to run a successful election campaign.

In turn, elected officials are loyal to their parties. Without loyalty, the odds of being re-elected are vanishingly small. Once elected, party politicians understand that if they behave contrary to the wishes of their party, their support, promotion, and funding will disappear, as will their chances of remaining in office. Keeping their jobs becomes a higher priority than doing their jobs. Hence, their fish-like behavior at the State of the Union Address.

Given this arrangement, it's clear that the mission of the parties is to seize power and hold onto it. They do this by narrowing the list of candidates to those who are loyal to the party. Money is the enabler that allows parties to accomplish this mission. With sufficient funding, parties can promote their chosen candidates and disparage opponents. The voting public is swamped with political ads and propaganda. Money can buy polls whose results indicate how and where to better direct the candidate's funding. Money can buy television ads, social media ads, billboard ads, mailings, podcast interviews, op-ed pieces, and so on. Money is the key.

Which brings us to Political Action Committees (PACs). Though a PAC may endorse specific candidates, a PAC is different from a political party. View a party as a group of people with a common philosophy, platform, or goal. You can liken a party to a fraternal club, an athletic team, or a religious organization. A party is a group of people with common interests. A PAC, on the other hand, is a collection of money, not a collection of people. For any given PAC, the money has a singular aim. You can generally see what that aim is by looking at the name of the PAC. Here are the names of a bunch of larger

PACs, as measured by money spent in the 2023-2024 election cycle:

- Air Line Pilots Assn
- America's Credit Unions
- American Crystal Sugar
- Blue Cross / Blue Shield
- Laborers Union
- National Assn of Realtors
- National Beer Wholesalers Assn
- National Education Assn

These PACs exist to raise money and fund their own interests. They will promote or disparage whichever candidate, class of candidates, proposed legislation, or ballot initiatives they believe will help or hurt them. PACs originated in the 1940's, mainly to represent the interests of labor unions. They have since expanded to represent the interests of corporations, trade associations, political parties, and political candidates.

"Super PACs" are permitted by law to raise and spend an unlimited amount of money on any candidate they choose. The only catch is that they must be *non-connected*, and their spending must be *independent*. *Non-connected* means they cannot be sponsored by a particular corporation or union. *Independent* means they cannot converse with the candidate's campaign committee when designing and running ads for that candidate. As we see from the plethora of campaign ads that directly promote or attack specific candidates, these are restrictions in name only.

Campaign finance laws were passed in the Federal Election Campaign Act of 1971 and amended in subsequent years. The campaign finance laws were enacted in response to the growing belief that elections could be bought. The laws specify which entities may contribute to election campaigns and what the limits of those contributions are. In 1974, the Federal Election Commission (FEC) was established by an act of Congress as an independent agency of the U.S. Government to monitor and enforce campaign finance laws. The FEC establishes bookkeeping requirements to ensure and enforce that the rules are followed.

Unfortunately, laws are only as strict as the legislators who enact them and the courts who interpret them. At present, as indicated above, the limits are large enough to drive a dump truck of cash through. The attempt to reform campaign finance in any meaningful way has failed.

And perhaps that's as it should be. In a nation founded on the concept of freedom, how do we justify a restriction on the freedom of citizens to spend their money promoting someone they like? Where and how do we draw the lines? Maybe we need to think like the Founders and have a bit more faith that **We the People** can discern fact from fancy. Since we already endure daily lives in which we are surrounded by promotions, pitches, and promises, let's resist the urge to have the Constitution play nanny as it tries to protect us from the inevitable. The dollars will fall where they will.

Instead, let's restrain the power of political parties by targeting their ability to control the selection of candidates. We'll cover that in the next chapter. But since we're discussing campaign finances, let's at least make sure the finances are being used for campaigns as intended by donors. Here's the start of

Article IV, Section 10 of the new Constitution, regarding election rules:

> *A Federal Election Commission (the Commission) shall be established by Congress to administer and enforce Federal campaign and election laws.*
>
> *Candidates for offices of President, Senator, and Representative shall submit to the Commission by the first day of December prior to that election year an application which shall include name, contact information, office sought, and required qualifications. Campaign donations shall be used exclusively for activities relating to the candidate's campaign in that election. Within 60 days following the general election, residual campaign donations shall be returned by the candidate's committee to campaign donors pro rata.*

This passage makes no explicit mention of parties or PACs, nor does it aim to destroy the ability of We the People to form groups with common interests. Parties have been with us since the founding of the country and will likely be with us until its demise. But let's see if we can break the grip that parties currently have over the selection of candidates and the control of elections. It would be fruitful if our officials could concentrate on doing the jobs they've been elected to do rather than glancing back to see whether their parties approve.

Finally, though the Constitution may remain mum on the existence and function of parties, there are revisions we can make to dial back the adversarial nature of parties. We elect Senators and Representatives with the expectation that they will work together in the spirit of civility to make our lives better. We want to see them cooperating and compromising, not fighting and pointing fingers. To quote Benjamin Franklin at the signing of the Declaration of Independence, "We must all hang together, or assuredly we shall all hang separately." The second clause of Article I, Section 7 currently reads,

> *Every Bill which shall have passed the House of Representatives and the Senate, shall, before it become a Law, be presented to the President of the United States;*

In the new Constitution, this clause reads,

> *Every Bill which shall have passed by two thirds of both the House of Representatives and the Senate, shall, before it become a Law, be presented to the President of the United States;*

The addition of the words *by two thirds of both* imposes the burden of cooperation and compromise. At present, Bills approved by just 51% of the Representatives and Senators, and presumably of the people, can be passed. Instead, Bills will require more thoughtful crafting to reflect the will of 67%, not just 51%.

One could argue that two thirds is an impossible requirement. Most legislation these days squeezes by with just 51% or 52% of the vote. Given the current composition of Congress, few bills will manage to get 67%. Legislation will be gridlocked.

Perhaps. But is gridlock much worse than where we

now stand? The current 51% threshold invites adversarial behavior, while a 67% requirement instead demands cooperation. The message is, "Learn to work together or prepare to perish together. Think of one another as family, not foe. If you can't get the job done, We the People will elect others who can. Your choice of the party over the people is no longer acceptable."

This wording revision leads to other changes. In particular, the Vice President, who continues to act as President of the Senate, will no longer have a tie-breaking vote. The clause in Article I, Section 3 no longer contains the words *unless they be equally divided*:

> *The Vice President of the United States shall be President of the Senate, but shall have no Vote.*

The power of the President to veto a bill still exists, still requires the Reconsideration of both Houses, and still requires the approval by two thirds of each house. However, the likelihood of a Presidential Veto succeeding is reduced significantly since both Houses will have already met the two thirds threshold. The President will need to be especially persuasive to convince at least some members of Congress to reverse their votes.

Elections

Some of us view civic responsibility as a requirement to rise from our easy chairs once every four years so we can go to the polls and vote for President. Those of us who are more civic minded rise every two years to vote for members of Congress. Even more committed are those who vote twice every two years, once in the Primary Election and again in the General Election. Part of the tradition of voting is to grumble about the list of choices from which we must choose. In general, the choices come from the major parties, as discussed in the previous chapter.

In this chapter, we present an alternative in which **We the People** have a greater say in deciding which candidates appear on the ballot. As a result, the influence of the parties is further reduced, and power is returned to the people. Unfortunately, greater involvement by the people means, well, greater involvement by the people. It means getting out of the easy chair more often. Some people will resist this requirement, preferring the simpler path of relying on the parties to do the hard work. In that way, they can merely pick one of the two choices approved by the parties and justifiably grumble. For the rest of us who are aching to have a greater say in the candidate-selection process and are willing to invest more of our time, this new process provides the opportunity.

Right off you should know that the extra voter effort comes in the form of three trips to the polls rather than two. Also, this new process expects and encourages voters to take a more active role in becoming acquainted with the candidates.

However, citizens do remain free to go to the polls or not, and to educate themselves or not, as their civic consciences dictate. We'll begin by describing the candidate selection process in broad strokes from the point of view of the candidate. Then we'll get into the details.

Suppose you want to run for Senator. You fill out a short form and submit it to the Federal Election Commission (FEC). In it, you provide your personal information including the office you seek, and your qualifications as required by the Constitution, such as age, address of residence, country of birth, and so on. While the FEC confirms the application, you pound the bricks, do interviews, give speeches, put up posters, run ads, swamp social media, and do whatever else you can to get your name out there. At this stage, the bar is low. You don't have to win; you must merely prove that you're a viable contender. In essence, this is a drive for the approval of people who will attest that they would *consider* voting for you. You pass around cards on which your name and office sought are printed, so the voters will remember you.

Conceptually, your aim is to gather a certain number of approvals to qualify. Logistically, you could do this by collecting signatures. However, signature collection is a messy business. To avoid the possibility of fake or duplicate signatures, an impartial official would need to reach out to each signer to make sure that the signature is valid. Such a process would be time-consuming, expensive, fraught with error, and a potential violation of privacy. Fortunately, the citizen identity validation process already exists in America in the form of voting polls. So, instead of providing signatures, the voters head to the polls for the first round of the candidate selection process.

Let's call this the *Qualification Election*. Each voter is given lists, compiled by the FEC, of registered applicants by office and is allowed to attest (check a box) for several candidates in each of the open offices that year. These are the candidates for whom the voter would *consider* voting, based on the limited candidate exposure to date. We use the word *several* here, but the word *field*, as in a horse race, is more apt. The *field* is the maximum number to whom you may attest for a given office. Here, we propose a field of eight for President, six for Senator, and for Representative a field of three times the number of Representatives in that State. For example, this means each voter can attest for up to six Senatorial candidates.

The number of attestations (checks) from the *Qualification Election* is tallied by candidate. Those who reach a threshold specified in the Constitution move on. The others are disqualified. The thresholds are determined by a Constitutional formula, which is a function of the office and State. As an example, to qualify for the office of Senator in Connecticut, you would have needed around 8,000 attestations in 2024.

Note that while the field for Senator is six, which means any given voter can attest to at most six Senatorial candidates, the number of candidates who qualify, i.e. pass the *Qualification Election*, may be more or less than six. Only Senatorial candidates who receive enough attestations to reach the Constitutional threshold move on.

As a candidate for Senator, suppose you get enough votes to stay in the race. Your next step is to contact the FEC with your campaign *docket*. This is a package you design to reveal yourself to the voters and to challenge your opponents. It consists of two parts:

1. The *Written Statement* is a few pages, no more than two thousand words, in which you lay out the reasons constituents should vote for you.

2. The *Challenge Questions* is a list of five questions you would like to pose to the opposing challengers for this office.

Once the FEC has gathered the dockets from all candidates, you are scheduled to do a video recording at an FEC office. The video recording consists of two parts:

1. The *Video Statement* is a short video, no longer than ten minutes, in which you visually present yourself.

2. The *Responses Video* is a recording in which you provide ad hoc responses to up to ten questions posed by your opponents, taking up to five minutes for each response.

Note that the questions asked are randomly selected for you by the FEC from the entire list of *Challenge Questions* provided by your opponents.

Once the FEC records these videos, it makes them and the *Written Statements* available online to the public. Note that the FEC plays no role in restricting what the candidates write or say, other than to truncate their responses to the limits indicated. Nor does it make any attempt to fact-check or fact-correct what is written or said. The responsibility for such assessments belongs to the voters and the press.

To get an idea how this works, imagine yourself as a voter going to a single FEC-maintained internet site to learn as much as possible about the candidates. The information comes from the candidates themselves through the process described above. You open your browser and navigate to the FEC site. Once at the site, you supply the year of the election and your State, for example:

Election year: 2028
State: MA

You are then presented a list of the Federal offices that have open seats in the given election year in that State:

Office: o President
o Senator
o Representative

Note that the small circles above are called *radio buttons* or *options*. You click one to fill in the circle to indicate your choice. Next, you see a menu of candidates for the office you selected, as well as three types of available information:

Senator: o John Smith o Frank Adams
o Mary Jones o Louise White

Show: o Written Statement
o Video Statement
o Responses Video

Pick a candidate and select the type of information you want to see. The *Written Statement*, as described above, is a few pages prepared by candidates in which they lay out the reasons you should vote for them. The *Video Statement* is a short recording, no longer than ten minutes, by the candidates in which they likewise present themselves. The *Responses Video* is a recording in which the candidates respond to ten questions posed by their opponents, taking up to five minutes for each response. If you choose *Responses Video*, you see a list of questions, for example,

Frank Adams responded to these questions:

- **What is your stance on immigration?**
- **Do you suggest any changes to our educational system?**
- **Where do you stand on the legality of abortion?**
- **What role should our country play in NATO?**
- (and so on…)

Note that these are just sample questions. Since the actual questions come from the candidate's *opponents*, they are likely to be more difficult.

Through such an internet site, you get to read and hear what candidates have to say on the issues and see how they present themselves when challenged. This may not give you a perfect view of the candidates, but it's quicker, deeper, and more encouraging than months of negative political campaign ads.

The second vote is held. This is the *Primary Election.* Voters go to the polls, are given a ballot that lists remaining candidates for each office. As described in an earlier chapter, the

Three-Star Voting method is used: Great (3), Good (2), Fair (1), or Poor (0). Voters can assign as few as zero and as many as three stars to each of the candidates. In general, voters will likely assign 3 stars to all candidates they find acceptable and leave the others at 0. However, voters are free to assign any of the numbers to any of the candidates. When the votes are tallied, the *field* of candidates with the most stars prevail. Again, the *field* for President is eight, for Senator is six, and for Representative is three times the number of Representatives in that State. The others are disqualified.

Suppose you're a candidate for Senator and are fortunate enough to be in the final field of six candidates. After the *Primary Election*, you're allowed the option of presenting a new campaign docket to the FEC. You may provide a new *Written Statement* and a new set of *Challenge Questions* for your opponents. Once the FEC has gathered the dockets, all candidates are again scheduled to do a video recording at an FEC office. As a candidate, you have the option of recording a second *Video Statement*, which will be made available by the FEC, along with your first. And you must record a second *Responses Video*, in which you again provide ad hoc responses to up to ten of the most recently submitted questions posed by your opponents. This set of responses is made available by the FEC, along with the first set.

Once the FEC gathers this information, they make it available online to the public. The nonpartisan FEC has no power to re-record or withdraw written or video statements once submitted or recorded.

The third vote is held. This is the *General Election*. Voters go to the polls, are given a ballot that lists the remaining fields of candidates for each office. The Three-Star Voting method is used. When the votes are tallied, the candidate with the most stars wins. In the case of Representatives, the number elected for a given State depends on the number of Reps apportioned for that State, with those having the most stars assigned the seats.

This is the general flow. Let's get down to specifics.

In the original Constitution, the States are assigned the power to conduct elections, according to Article I, Section 4:

> *The Times, Places and Manner of holding Elections for Senators and Representatives, shall be prescribed in each State by the Legislature thereof; but the Congress may at any time by Law make or alter such Regulations.*

The States will continue to control and conduct the *Election* process. The control over the new procedural steps described above involving the *Candidates* is controlled at the federal level. As mentioned in the previous chapter, the FEC already exists for the purposes of monitoring campaign finance laws through candidate committees. We include some wording in the Constitution for them to direct these new efforts. Note that the additional responsibilities of the FEC are designed to be strictly administrative and hence resistant to partisan influence. Here's the wording under Article IV, Section 10 in the new Constitution:

> *A Federal Election Commission (the Commission) shall be established by Congress to administer and enforce Federal campaign and election laws.*

Candidates for offices of President, Senator, and Representative shall submit to the Commission by the first day of December prior to that election year an application which shall include name, contact information, office sought, and required qualifications. Campaign donations shall be used exclusively for activities relating to the candidate's campaign in that election. Within 60 days following the general election, residual campaign donations shall be returned by the candidate's committee to campaign donors pro rata.

By the first of January of the election year, the Commission shall publish the names and offices of Candidates so Registered.

On the first Tuesday following the first Monday of February of the election year, the Qualification Election shall be held, in which Voters shall from the lists of Registered Candidates attest to as many as eight for President, six times the number of open Senate seats in the State for Senator, and three times the number of Representatives apportioned to the State for Representative. Candidates qualify for the Primary Election who receive sufficient attestations, the number so required depending on the office sought, upon the United States and separate State Populations from the most recent ten-year Enumeration, and upon the most recent Representative apportionment by State: for President, the product of 0.002 and the U.S. Population; for Representative, the product of 0.005 and the State Population divided by the number of the State's Representatives; for Senator, the product of 0.005, the State Population, and the square-root of the number of Representatives apportioned to the State, then divided by the number of that State's Representatives.

To get an idea of the number of attestations required to qualify, an election held in 2024 would require about 700,000 attestations for President, about 3,500 for Representative, and about 3,000 for a Wyoming Senator -- 8,000 for a Connecticut Senator -- 27,000 for a California Senator.

Qualified Candidates shall submit to the Commission by the first day of March of that election year a written campaign statement designated for public release, that statement being rendered in plain text and being no longer than two thousand words, and a written list of five questions to be posed to opposing Candidates.

By the first day of April of that election year, Candidates shall sit for video recording of campaign remarks, such recording administered under the direction of the Commission, having a common backdrop for all Candidates, with no music or special effects, and lasting no more than ten minutes. At the same sitting, the Candidate shall be recorded responding to ten, or fewer if unavailable, written questions from opponent Candidates, those questions selected randomly by and known only to the Commission, its only discretion being to remove perceived duplicates. The Candidate is allowed sixty seconds from receipt of each question to respond, and each response may last no more than five minutes.

By the first day of May of that election year, the Federal Election Commission shall make such written statements, video statements, and video responses freely and readily available to all U.S. citizens.

Not all citizens have internet access but more than 90% do. For those who don't, internet access is generally available at local libraries. The FEC can also arrange broadcasts of candidate videos on local public service television channels on an announced schedule. Written statements can be made available at libraries or Post Offices.

On the first Tuesday following the first Monday of June of the election year, the Primary Election shall be held, in which Voters shall award each Qualified Candidate 3 (Great), 2 (Good), 2 (Fair), or 0 (Poor). Candidates qualify for the General Election whose total tally for President is in the top eight, for Senator is in the top six times the number of open Senate seats for the State, and for Representative is in the top three times the number of Representatives apportioned to that State.

After the Primary election, there remain no more than eight candidates for President, six candidates for each Senator position, and up to three times the number of Representatives that the state has been apportioned. For example, California, the most populous state, currently has 52 Representatives. Since the total number of U.S. Representatives is being reduced in the new Constitution from 435 to 200, California will have about 23 Representatives. As such, the Primary election in California will reduce the number of eligible candidates to no more than 69. For small states that have a single Representative, the Primary election will narrow the list of candidates to three.

The period between June and November allows candidates on the General ballot time to continue to present themselves to the voting public.

> *By the first day of July of that election year, remaining Candidates shall at their option submit to the Commission revisions to their written campaign statement, and to their written list of five questions to be posed to opposing Candidates.*

> *By the first day of August of that election year, the Candidate shall be recorded responding to ten, or fewer if unavailable, revised questions from opponent Candidates. At the same sitting, Candidates shall at their option sit for a revised video recording of campaign remarks.*

> *By the first day of September of that election year, the Federal Election Commission shall make both original and revised written statements, video statements, and video responses freely and readily available to all U.S. citizens.*

> *By the first day of October of that election year, Candidates for President shall select a Vice President whose name shall join theirs on the General Election ballot. Having one's name on that ballot as President shall not preclude the Candidate having his or her name once or more on the ballot as Vice President.*

On the first Tuesday following the first Monday of November of the election year, the General Election for offices of President/Vice President, Senators, and Representatives shall be held, in which Voters shall award each Candidate 3 (Great), 2 (Good), 2 (Fair), or 0 (Poor). Candidates with the highest tallies shall fill the open seats. If two Senate seats are open for a State, the elected Senator with highest tally shall choose the seat to fill.

Another way to get to see the candidates in action is by watching televised debates, especially if you want to see how they react to difficult questions and accusations. In recent years, stream/broadcast debates have not drawn big audiences, the complaints of prospective viewers being that the candidates don't answer the questions, the tone of the debates is too negative, and the questions are too grand for the allotted time. Such criticisms don't denigrate the concept of debates, only the way the debates are currently staged. The well-attended Lincoln-Douglas debates were about six hours in duration. Perhaps there's some happy middle ground for today's citizens.

Curious voters will still be free to immerse themselves in newspaper commentaries, news programs, and social media to explore the opinions of others. Fans of specific candidates may choose to write op-ed pieces, stage rallies, or pay for billboards and TV time to promote their candidates. But only from debates and FEC-managed candidate statements and videos will you be getting information from the unbridled horse's mouth.

Electoral Votes

When the delegates of the Constitutional Convention were faced with the issue of appointing a President, the question that arose was who should have a voice in that decision. If the States are to choose, then each State should get a vote. If the People are to choose, then each citizen should get a vote. Considering arguments on each side, the delegates settled on a compromise. They decided that both the States and the People should have a voice in choosing the President.

Tying this solution to the work already done for Congressional representation, they created an *electoral college*, which consists of as many *electors* as there are Senators and Representatives in Congress. Today, there are 100 Senators and 435 Representatives, so there are 535 electors. The 23rd Amendment to the Constitution grants Washington DC three electors for the Presidential election, reasoning that if DC were a State, it would have two Senators and at least one Representative. Thus, there are currently 538 electors in the electoral college.

The Constitution grants States latitude to decide how their electors will vote. Typically, States assign their electoral votes to the Presidential candidate who wins the popular vote in that State. The only exceptions are Maine and Nebraska, which allocate their electoral votes proportionally based on the popular vote within their respective States. The electoral college arrangement has some interesting effects. For example, if the voting for two candidates in California is very close, say 50.2% vs. 49.8%, the one with the slight lead gets 54 electoral votes while the other gets none. Because of this all-or-nothing nature, candidates do their campaigning most heavily in States whose results are predicted to be close, ignoring States that poll strongly one way or the other. States where the polling is tight have come to be known as *Battleground* or *Swing* States because it is in these states that the candidates wage their most ambitious campaigns, and where elections are often won or lost.

To avoid this lopsided behavior, arguments have been made to replace the electoral vote system with popular vote. In the 59 Presidential elections to date, 54 of the winners have also won the popular vote, so the results from such a change would mostly be the same. Generally, those who argue about keeping the electoral college system are often those who would benefit at that moment from the electoral system. The five Presidents who lost the popular vote but won the Presidency are in this camp. Conversely, those who argue about eliminating the electoral college system are often those who would thereby benefit.

Our argument for electing the President based on the popular vote is that the President represents all the people equally so everyone should have a voice in his or her election. The argument is simple and nonpartisan, as it should be. The new Constitution makes the change in Article II, Section 1, removing the discussion of Electors and replacing it with this:

> *The executive Power shall be vested in a President of the United States of America. He shall hold his Office during the Term of four Years, and, together with the Vice President, chosen for the same Term, be elected by the citizens of the United States and of the District constituting the seat of Government of the United States.*

Term Limits

In the original Constitution, none of the officials were limited by the number of terms they could serve. A President could serve any number of four-year terms; a Senator could serve any number of six-year terms; and a Representative could serve any number of two-year terms.

In a nation of free citizens, this makes perfect sense. If We the People approve of a particular official, and if that official wants to run for the same office repeatedly, we should be free to reelect him or her any number of times. However, the 22nd Amendment changed this by limiting the President to two four-year terms. The Amendment was ratified in 1951 because of Franklin D. Roosevelt's four terms in office, the fourth term of which he served only three months before he died. Friends and foes of FDR felt four terms were too many. Friends felt such a lengthy reign was not good for the President's health; foes felt it was not good for the country, resulting in an inevitable and unwelcome concentration of power.

The traditional perspective of representative government in America is anecdotal. The farmer sets down his plowshare and travels to Washington to do his part for the country. He returns home to farm and family a few years later, having fulfilled his public duty. The farmer has put his own life on hold, sacrificing his time and energy for the country's welfare. This is why we speak of public *service*, not public employment.

In practice, this anecdote is off the mark. Once Senators and Representatives land their positions, they tend to hold onto them. As professional politicians, they seem to have little desire to move back to the plowshare. The position becomes their occupation, not a temporary sacrifice, and they will often do what it takes to hold onto it. Perhaps, as Lord Acton put it, power corrupts. While many if not most of our Senators and Representatives enter the fray with lofty ideals, their principles erode over time at the altars of self-interest and pragmatism. The American people are not blind to this. Polls show that the approval rating of Congress has been stuck below 30% since 2010.

You can't blame politicians for wanting to hold onto a career that brings them fame, power, and wealth. But we may be able to redirect their priorities by instituting term limits, as was done for Presidents. Such a change is written into the new Constitution. Left to their own devices, members of Congress have never shown a willingness to press for term limits. The act would be self-destructive. Here's what the new Constitution mandates:

- Two four-year terms for President (no change)
- Two six-year terms for Senator
- Four two-year terms for Representative

By limiting their terms, the new Constitution makes clear that our officials should concentrate their efforts on getting the job done, not on getting re-elected. The message is: do what's good for the people of this country and then with our gratitude go home to your real job.

Per the current Constitution, Supreme Court Justices are appointed by the President and granted a life term. This is because there exists a conflict between the concept of running for office and the concept of dispensing blind justice. The former requires Justices to appeal to popular sentiment, while the latter requires them to interpret the law despite popular sentiment. To remove the need for Justices to run for office, the President appoints them for life as vacancies appear, subject to Senate approval. The rationale for a life term is that Justices thereby have the independence needed to make impartial rulings without fear of being removed. Life terms also provide a degree of predictability and stability in court rulings.

That's the theory. In practice, Supreme Court Justices can be as partisan as the President and members of Congress. Since the job of the Supreme Court is to interpret the law, and since each of the nine Justices is assumed to be an educated and respected expert in the study of law, you would expect that their opinions would generally be unanimous, or nearly so. In the 2023-2024 Supreme Court Docket, eleven of the cases were decided by 9-0 or 8-1 decisions. The other nineteen were decided by 5-4 or 6-3 decisions, with consistent Justices on opposing sides. It seems the cases were being decided by partisan politics, not by careful legal analysis. To anticipate a Justice's vote in a case before the Supreme Court, you may not need to understand the legal underpinnings of the case at hand, only whether the Justice's undergarments are red or blue.

Such partisanship is possible because the approval of a nominated Justice requires only a majority vote in the Senate. If the Senate is controlled by the same party as the President and if partisan politics are valued more highly than ethics, then it's straightforward to appoint a Justice who delivers what the party wants: The President nominates the partisan Justice and the Senate approves the nomination.

The problem with having Justices that are partisan is that

they have the motivation and ability to act beyond their Constitutional mandate of *interpreting* the law to one of *establishing* the law in favor of their partisan views. Then, Lady Justice is no longer blind. Life terms only exacerbate the problem. As with Congressmen and Presidents, power tends to corrupt. Again, a shorter term can force these officials to keep their focus on their country, not on personal views.

To overcome these deficits in the existing system, the new Constitution proposes several changes.

First, the number of Supreme Court Justices is permanently codified at nine. Because the number is not specified in the current Constitution, Congress has been able to change the number of Justices, as it has done from time to time, causing the Court to range from five to ten Justices. Since 1869, the number of sitting Justices has been nine. The new Constitution makes number nine explicit.

Second, a nominated Justice must be confirmed by a two-thirds majority rather than a simple majority. This change makes it nearly impossible to appoint a partisan Justice. Justices who display any leanings other than to a fair interpretation of the law will likely be rejected by at least a third of the Senators.

Third, a Supreme Court Justice is replaced every two years. A new Justice is nominated by the President on the 1st of March of each even year. The odd year is not used because a new President may have been in office for only a month. When the Justice is confirmed, he or she fills a vacancy if it exists, or else replaces the Justice who has been longest on the bench. A past Justice cannot be re-appointed. Thus, the longest term for a Supreme Court Justice is 18 years. When a vacancy does occur, through death, retirement, impeachment, or other cause, the vacancy remains until the next scheduled nomination.

Fourth, the Chief Justice is selected by the Court itself. The Chief Justice has several responsibilities beyond those held by Associate Justices. For example, the Chief is responsible for assigning cases, deciding who writes the majority opinion, administrative management of the federal judicial system, presiding over oral court proceedings, and so on. In all these matters, the nine members of the Court are in a better position to decide who would best serve as Chief Justice to handle these tasks than are the President or Congress. The Court may reassign the office of Chief Justice at their discretion.

In the current Constitution, all these matters are covered lightly, if at all:

Article II, Section 2: [The President] shall nominate, and by and with the Advice and Consent of the Senate, shall appoint ... Judges of the supreme Court.

Article III, Section 1: The judicial Power of the United States, shall be vested in one supreme Court, and in such inferior Courts as the Congress may from time to time ordain and establish. The Judges, both of the supreme and inferior Courts, shall hold their Offices during good Behavior, and shall, at stated Times, receive for their Services, a Compensation, which shall not be diminished during their Continuance in Office.

Here is the revised wording in the new Constitution:

Article II, Section 2: On the 1st day of March of each Year wholly divisible by two, the President shall nominate, and by and with the Advice and Consent of the Senate, shall appoint one Judge to the supreme Court, provided two thirds of the Senators present concur. No Judge having previously served on the supreme Court shall be reappointed. The Judge so appointed shall fill an open vacancy if one exists, else shall replace the Justice having served longest on the supreme Court.

Article III, Section 1: The judicial Power of the United States, shall be vested in one supreme Court having nine members one of whom shall be designated as Chief Justice by its members, and in such inferior Courts as the Congress may from time to time ordain and establish. The Judges, both of the supreme and inferior Courts, shall hold their Offices during good Behavior, and shall, at stated Times, receive for their Services, a Compensation, which shall not be diminished during their Continuance in Office. When vacancies happen in the supreme Court, they shall remain unfilled until the biannual Presidential appointment and Senate confirmation.

Let's take a moment to recap. For two and a half centuries, the Constitution has shown itself to be a durable document. Still, human nature being what it is, holes in the Constitution have been uncovered and exploited in ways that have violated the Constitution's intent. Now, we are taking the opportunity to plug those holes. We do this knowing that words alone do not make the Constitution. The Founders understood this as well. For such an ambitious undertaking, the Constitution they drafted was brief. “Let’s keep it broad,” they must have reasoned, “and leave it to honorable posterity to make it work.”

As we insert and alter wording, it’s natural to wonder what new holes are being introduced and what old holes remain. While pressing forward in the mission to fill the holes, we acknowledge a reliance on the goodwill of our successors.

Let’s take an example. Suppose the President nominates a Supreme Court Justice on March 1st of the Presidential election year. Suppose the Senate Majority Leader, who is responsible for scheduling Senate debates and votes, does not like the President’s choice. Concerned that the Senate may vote to approve the nominated Justice despite his disapproval, the Majority Leader refuses to include in the Senate’s legislative agenda an opportunity to debate and vote on this nomination as mandated by the Constitution. Instead, he decides to postpone the vote for eleven months until a different President and a different set of Senators have been elected.

We could include some wording in this new Constitution that might fill this “hole” by requiring that the process be expeditious. For example, if the vote is not taken within six months, that Justice is automatically approved. However, then the President might use this provision to game the system. If the Senate Majority Leader is in cahoots with the President, the President could nominate someone he likes but who would never normally be confirmed. The Majority Leader can then hold up the vote for six months, so the nominee is automatically approved.

No matter how carefully the Constitution is crafted, those who value their own interests above those of the country will always be able to find ways to bend words to their will and violate the Constitution’s intent. This is the reason all officials of the U.S. Government are sworn to uphold the Constitution. The assumption has always been that when honorable people give their word, they will abide by it. The Founders relied on that.

Experience has shown that some of our elected officials do not honor their pledge to uphold the Constitution. Still, all hope is not lost. If **We the People** are willing to recognize and abhor the dishonor, we shall always have the power and responsibility to vote them out of office.

Emoluments and Lobbyists

Presidents, Congressmen, and Supreme Court Justices, through the power vested in them by the Constitution, can influence the success and failure of individuals, businesses, and nations. The laws and agreements that are legislated, executed, and adjudicated by the three branches of the U.S. Government are intended to benefit the citizens of the United States. However, in the short term these policies may help or hurt some parties more than others. Those with a vested interest in the outcome of Government policies will naturally take whatever action they can to influence these policies. The act of bribing government officials to influence their actions is as timeless as the concept of government itself.

While bribing officials may be a common practice in some countries, the United States has generally been intolerant of the practice. In the Constitution, the word *Emoluments* is mentioned three times. Technically, the word *Emoluments* refers to salary, fees, profit, or returns from employment or office. Such fees open the door to bribes. Here are the uses of that word in the Constitution:

Article I, Section 6:

No Senator or Representative shall, during the Time for which he was elected, be appointed to any civil Office under the Authority of the United States, which shall have been created, or the ***Emoluments*** *whereof shall have been increased during such time; and no Person holding any Office under the United States, shall be a Member of either House* *during his Continuance in Office.*

Article I, Section 9:

No Title of Nobility shall be granted by the United States: And no Person holding any Office of Profit or Trust under them, shall, without the Consent of the Congress, accept of any present, ***Emolument****, Office, or Title, of any kind whatever, from any King, Prince, or foreign State.*

Article II, Section 1:

The President shall, at stated Times, receive for his Services, a Compensation, which shall neither be increased nor diminished during the Period for which he shall have been elected, and he shall not receive within that Period any other ***Emolument*** *from the United States, or any of them.*

The Founders were concerned that officials, given their power, could be bought. In these passages, they politely dance around the subject, perhaps figuring that the officials will get the point and honor it. Sadly, today's honor code is not what it was in the 1780's. Most of our public officials leave office with far more wealth than they had when they entered. The wealth comes in the form of gifts, advances for book deals, trading based on insider information, campaign donations, the occasional gold bar, and more. In whatever form, the recipients generally believe that they deserve the wealth, and that their acceptance of it does not influence their ability to fairly perform their duties.

Whether or not that's true, the aim of the Constitution is not to enrich government officials. The obvious conflict of interest that Emoluments raise is too important to ignore. In the new Constitution, the issue is handled directly. Basically, anything an official acquires due to the office, other than salary, must be surrendered to the U.S. Treasury. If there's the slightest scent of corruption, such as any appearance of conflict of interest, the amount is doubled. Within one month of taking office, officials must present to the Federal Election Commission a private accounting of their wealth as of the date they are approved or elected to office. Within one month after leaving office, they must provide a similar accounting of their wealth as of that termination date. The FEC compares the assessments to determine where wealth has increased due in any manner to the office being held. Values that likely would not otherwise have accrued must be remitted to the U.S. Treasury within 180 days. Values received that show any appearance of quid pro quo or attempts to conceal are so indicated in the FEC assessment and must be doubled when being remitted. Here is the new wording:

> *Article IV, Section 11:*
>
> *Within thirty days of taking office, each President, Senator, Representative, and Supreme Court Justice shall present to the Federal Election Commission an accounting of the value of his estate as of the date of approval, confirmation, or election. Within thirty days of the final day in office, he shall provide a final accounting of the value of his estate as of the date of termination, including amounts accrued, pledged, or constructively owned but held by others, and an accounting of the value of perquisites while in office beyond the Compensation for his Services as ascertained by Law. Within 90 days, the Federal Election Commission shall provide an as-*

sessment of the amount deemed attributable to the office held. The amount shall be remitted by the ex-official or his estate to the U.S. Treasury within 180 days of the assessment. The portion of the amount held by others or having appearance of quid pro quo shall be so indicated in the assessment, and its value doubled upon remission. Penalties from these assessments shall not extend further than these remissions, but the Party so penalized shall nevertheless be liable and subject to Indictment, Trial, Judgment and Punishment, according to Law.

The word *pledged* refers to wealth promised to the official but not yet paid, i.e. intended to be paid after the official leaves office. The term *constructively owned* refers to the situation in which an official has stashed his wealth under the names of his children, spouse, siblings, friends, or other associates, but still retains some control over it. The term *perquisites* refers to items provided by foreign nations, corporations, wealthy individuals, or others for use by the official before, during or after his term in office.

We shouldn't discuss the possibility of bribing officials without mentioning lobbyists. Lobbyists are individuals and groups hired to influence government officials. Their goal is to persuade the officials to make decisions and pass laws that work in the favor of their employer. Likewise, nations seek treaties and policies that benefit them. In this sense, their ambassadors often serve the function of lobbyists.

Since lobbyists are the individuals most highly motivated to influence our government officials, it's reasonable to look at them when seeking ways to discourage bad behavior, such as bribing. One could suggest that the practice itself of lobbying should be illegal. However, if the lobbyists who understand their industries or countries better than most people aren't allowed to educate our government officials, who will? Though lobbyists have axes to grind, their axes may be ground in a way that benefits the citizens of our country. Just as our citizens are free to lobby their government officials, so should corporate, union, or foreign lobbyists. The problem lies not in the lobbying, but in the bribing. The above Section handles that.

Presidential Powers

Executive Orders are meant to be directives by the President to manage the operation of the Federal Government. The power of the President to issue Executive Orders can be inferred from the Constitution in Article II, Section 1:

The executive Power shall be vested in a President of the United States of America.

and in Article II, Section 3:

... he shall take Care that the Laws be faithfully executed ...

No other wording in the Constitution relates to Executive Orders. In practice, the purpose of Executive Orders has been to assist the President in the execution of laws passed by Congress. Executive Orders allow the President and his departments or agencies to deal with the details of executing laws to achieve their legislated intent.

The purpose of Executive Orders is not to establish new laws, whose passage is the sole responsibility of Congress. Each Executive Order is expected to be justified in support of clarifying a particular existing law. The exception to this is when the Order includes the phrase *under the authority vested in me by the Constitution*, which implies the justification for the Order can be found in the Constitution's appointment of Presidential power rather than in a particular law.

The Supreme Court has the power to overturn Executive Orders in rulings on cases that come before them. Congress can overturn an Executive Order by passing a law that negates the Order. Congress can also indirectly revoke an Order by not providing the funding required to support it. A President can cancel Executive Orders at any time, whether issued by him or by a predecessor.

Until Abraham Lincoln became President, the average number of Executive Orders issued by a President was 10. From Teddy Roosevelt through Joe Biden, the average number was 697. Just from the numbers alone, it's clear that Presidents have gotten more heavily involved in the process of defining the details of legislation. Conversely, Congress has willingly relinquished this aspect of its Constitutional responsibility. While this surrender of duty may ease the burden on Congress, the effect can be somewhat chaotic. In general, each new President begins his term by repealing many or most of the Executive Orders of his predecessor. In other words, Congress has allowed some laws to be fluid enough that each President can reshape them to suit himself. From a Constitutional perspective, this is inappropriate since making law is the job of Congress, not the President.

In the new Constitution, Executive Orders are permitted but discouraged. The task of clarifying the workings of law is returned to Congress. Here's how it works.

When an Executive Order is issued, it does not take effect until approved by the Senate by a two-thirds majority. The President may repeal an Executive Order at any time, whether he issued it or not. The Senate may likewise repeal an Executive Order, even if they have previously approved it, provided they have a two-thirds majority. The President is free to issue the Executive Order again at a future date.

Here's an additional sentence in Article I, Section 3 of the new Constitution:

The Senate shall have the Power to repeal Executive Orders with the Concurrence of two thirds of the Members present.

and revised wording in Article II, Section 3:

...; he shall Commission all the Officers of the United States; he shall take Care that the Laws be faithfully executed and shall issue Executive Orders in furtherance of such duty that have the force of Law provided two thirds of the Senators present concur; he shall have Power to repeal Executive Orders.

In addition to issuing Executive Orders, the President currently has the power to grant Pardons per Article II, Section 2 of the original Constitution:

... and he shall have Power to grant Reprieves and Pardons for Offences against the United States, except in Cases of Impeachment.

The ability to grant Pardons was assigned as a final safeguard against a judicial system that might fail in some cases, causing an innocent individual to be unfairly convicted or sentenced. Experience has now shown that the power to Pardon can and has been abused. Presidents have used the power to provide "get out of jail free" cards to their friends, families, and cronies. The only two Presidents who granted no Pardons were the two who died early in office, William Henry Harrison and James A. Garfield. While many of us may know people in jail that we'd like to set free, the power to Pardon was not assigned as a bonus to the President. In the new Constitution, the ability to Pardon is removed from the President and assigned to the Supreme Court. Since the presumed injustice arises from within their branch, they should be tasked with righting the wrong. In addition to removing the Presidential Pardon passage from Article II, Section 2, this new passage is included in Article III, Section 2:

> *The supreme Court, with Concurrence of two thirds of its members, shall have Power to grant Reprieves and Pardons for Offences against the United States, except in Cases of Impeachment.*

National Debt

Since we'll be using specific numbers to make our point, let's select a particular moment in time. There's no time like the present. Let's pick January 1, 2025.

On this date, the national debt was $36.1 trillion. The population of the United States was approximately 341 million. Doing the division, we see that the debt was $105,865 per person.

Let's suppose you're a member of a family of four. Your family's portion of the debt is $423,460 (4 times $105,865). If you mortgaged this amount for your home, the number might not scare you. After all, if pressed by the bank, you can always sell the house and use the proceeds to repay the loan. In the case of the national debt, however, there is no house. The money has been borrowed and spent. Nothing remains but the memories and the interest payments on the outstanding debt.

Speaking of interest payments, the interest rate on Treasury Notes, which the Federal Government issues to fund the national debt, was around 4.5% during January 2025. If we apply that rate for the debt owed by the family of four, we get $19,056, which is the annual interest payment owed by that family for their share of the national debt. Put another way, $19,056 is the portion of taxes paid by that family each year to pay interest on that family's share of the national debt. The money goes to the investors, local and foreign, who prop up our country with their money to keep it financially afloat.

The debt, $36.1 trillion, is money spent by our government that we didn't have, which is the definition of debt, presumably to benefit the people of the United States currently alive. Since the government didn't have the money, the benefits we received must be paid for by our children and grandchildren. Likely our hypothetical family of four has no plans to dip into savings or salary to pay their $423,460 share. Their grandchildren will have to deal with it.

If you manage your own finances, you'll recognize a degree of irresponsibility by the federal government to be carrying so much debt. Though guilty of causing the debt, Congress recognizes the problem and knows that their spending must be reined in. In 1917, Congress passed the Second Liberty Bond Act, introducing a *debt ceiling*. Such a ceiling prohibits Congress from spending too much and going too far into debt. Unfortunately, it's simple enough for Congress to pass legislation that increases the debt ceiling, which they've done more than one hundred times since 1917.

In an earlier chapter, we talked about inflation. Before we come down too hard on Congress, inflation would seemingly require the debt ceiling to be increased, simply because dollars can buy less over time. Let's look at the numbers since 1917.

Start of	Debt in $Billions	Population	Gold ($/ounce)	Debt per capita (ounce)
1920	26	106,021,537	21	11.678
1930	17	122,775,046	21	6.594
1940	49	132,164,569	35	10.593
1950	275	151,325,798	40	45.432
1960	295	179,323,175	37	44.461
1970	377	203,302,031	39	47.548
1980	879	226,542,199	595	6.521
1990	3,123	248,709,873	386	32.531
2000	5,950	281,421,906	282	74.974
2010	12,394	308,745,538	1083	37.067
2020	22,030	331,449,281	1520	43.727
2025	36,100	341,000,000	2624	40.345

Look at the bottom row, which shows values as of the start of 2025. The Debt was $36.1 trillion, the population approximately 341 million, and the price of gold $2624 per ounce. We showed above that the per capita Debt is $105,865, which we got from dividing the total Debt by the total population. If we then divide this number by the price of gold ($2624), we get 40.345, the value in the last column. The Debt is 40.345 ounces of gold (or $105,865) per person at the start of 2025. In other words, this table transforms the Debt in the second column by considering both the population (third column) and the value of the dollar (fourth column) to get the Debt in ounces of gold per person (fifth column).

The results are revealing. While the second column [Debt in $Billions] shows our debt growing out of control over time, the rightmost column [Debt per capita (ounce)] shows that this is not so. In fact, our debt has been out of control since

1950. If the government had asked a family in 1950 to remit 45.432 ounces of gold per family member to pay off the national debt, their reaction and their ability to pay would likely be about the same as it would be today: "No way."

Two numbers in the rightmost column, specifically the ones for 1980 and 2000, require some explanation as they appear to buck the trend. The 6.521 value in 1980 is an outlier because the United States came off the gold standard in 1971. You can see the value of the dollar plummet relative to gold from 1970 ($39 per ounce) to 1980 ($595 per ounce). Though the total Debt continued to increase ($377 billion to $879 billion), the holders of that Debt found themselves being repaid in dollars that had significantly lower buying power than the dollars they had loaned the government. The other outlier, 74.974 in 2000, was the result of a strong dollar and a weakening demand for gold during the Clinton years.

Let's look at the Debt in a different but common way, namely how it stacks up against Gross Domestic Product (GDP). GDP is a measure of the total economic activity in the U.S. for a given year. Think of it as the value of goods the people of this country produce in that year.

Start of	Debt in $Billions	Gross Domestic Product in $Billions	Debt to GDP	Population	Gold ($/oz)	GDP Per Capita (oz)
1920	26	89	0.292	106,021,537	21	39.974
1930	17	90	0.189	122,775,046	21	34.907
1940	49	101	0.485	132,164,569	35	21.834
1950	275	300	0.917	151,325,798	40	49.562
1960	295	543	0.543	179,323,175	37	81.839
1970	377	1,076	0.350	203,302,031	39	135.708
1980	879	2,863	0.307	226,542,199	595	21.240
1990	3,123	5,963	0.524	248,709,873	386	62.113
2000	5,950	10,290	0.578	281,421,906	282	129.661
2010	12,394	14,990	0.824	308,745,538	1083	44.830
2020	22,030	20,930	1.053	331,449,281	1520	41.544
2024	34,191	29,184	1.172	335,900,000	2064	42.094

Notice that the bottom row is labeled 2024, not 2025. That's because the GDP for 2025 was unknown as of this writing (December 2025). The Debt, Population, and Gold Price figures for the last row have also been revised from the previous table to reflect the start of 2024, not 2025.

The fourth column is the ratio of Debt to GDP. Since we're comparing dollars each year to dollars in the same year, there's no need to convert to ounces of gold. This table shows the national Debt, as measured against GDP, increasing since 1980. Values greater than 1 indicate that Debt exceeds GDP. Such values mean that we would all have to work more than a year to generate enough wealth to pay off the Debt.

The point of this discussion is to make clear that the nation is carrying a Debt that is large and seemingly out of control. We will leave to the macroeconomists an explanation of how a country's excess debt can harm the people of the country. Even if the Debt was harmless, or if we rationalized that the harm would not materialize until we were long gone, the fact that our leaders are unable to control their spending suggests that the Constitution should weigh in.

To do so, we need to understand the nature of debt. Why do we borrow? In our daily personal or business lives, we borrow because we're building for tomorrow and we lack the cash to get started today. For example, we borrow to buy or build a house or a business. The idea is that future earnings, from the homeowner or business owner, will be used to repay the debt. Our country, on the other hand, is not a cash-strapped pioneer. It already has a source of money, namely its citizens, as taxpayers. If our nation needs money to perform its functions, or even to build something new, like aircraft carriers or rockets to Mars, it simply includes these items in the budget and taxes us accordingly.

The problem is that we generally like to see the Government spend money to benefit us, but we don't like to see our taxes go up. Our Senators and Representatives, in turn, recognize that if they don't cater to our seemingly contradictory desires, we will vote them out. Hence the Debt, and hence the need for the Constitution to require proper fiscal management.

Given that Congress can use taxation to raise money as needed, we might propose that no Debt at all should be allowed. What's needed is good planning. However, an argument can be made that if an emergency arises, Debt may be necessary to raise the funds to address the need. But isn't this the exact argument that should be made for maintaining a Surplus rather than a Debt? Isn't it fiscally responsible to keep some funds in the kitty for a rainy day? A budget that is responsible should have the foresight to set aside a little extra rather than expecting to borrow.

The Constitution can't see the future, so it shouldn't handcuff Congress too tightly. But history suggests that Federal spending needs to be reined in. Let's impose a Debt Ceiling that gives a little room, but not too much. If the current Debt is $105,865 or 40.345 ounces of gold per person (and four times that for a family of four), perhaps one-tenth that number would be a reasonable maximum. Let's set the Debt Ceiling at 4 Goldars (described in an earlier chapter) per capita. In dollars, the Debt Ceiling can be computed as the population as of the most recent Census times the current Goldar value. For example, in 2024 the Debt Ceiling would be $684 billion (331,449,281 times 2064). While we're at it, let's be optimistic and hope that Congress aims for a Surplus rather than a Debt. Being wildly optimistic, let's prevent Congress from setting aside too big a Surplus, which would benefit future citizens at the expense of current citizens. Let's use the same amount as a Surplus Floor.

Finally, if the future Debt Ceiling is 4 Goldars, but our current Debt is 40.345 Goldars, we need to suggest a repayment scheme that will pay off the debt. Twenty years seems a reasonable timeframe. Less would be a hardship for current citizens. More would be unfair to future citizens who have not realized the benefits of the past expenditures that created the Debt. In other words, we'll chip away at the Debt, repaying 1/20th of it each year.

Here's the new wording in Article 1, Section 9:

No Money shall be drawn from the Treasury to bring the

Debt of the United States, nor deposited to the Treasury to bring the Surplus of the United States, to more than four Goldars times the population as of the most recent ten-year Enumeration. The exception is that from the twenty-year period from 20xx to 20yy, the Debt may be as high as the Enumeration population times the greater of four or the product of (20yy-yyyy) times 40.345 divided by 20, where yyyy is the year of withdrawal.

Capitalism

At the start of 2025, there were 902 billionaires in the United States. The wealthiest American was Elon Musk, whose wealth was estimated at $400 billion. That's a lot of people with a lot of money. Is this normal, or is there a trend taking place at the top of the wealth spectrum in the U.S.? Here's a table with some values from the past 50 years.

Start of	Number of American Billionaires	Wealthiest American	His Wealth ($Billion)	Gold Price ($/ounce)	His Wealth (Million ounces)
1975	1	Daniel Ludwig	1	190	5.26
1980	13	Daniel Ludwig	2	850	2.35
1985	13	Sam Walton	2.8	308	9.09
1990	66	John Kluge	5.6	400	14.00
1995	94	Bill Gates	12.9	383	33.68
2000	360	Bill Gates	60	285	210.53
2005	341	Bill Gates	46.5	430	108.14
2010	404	Bill Gates	54	1100	49.09
2015	536	Bill Gates	76	1190	63.87
2020	614	Jeff Bezos	113	1520	74.34
2025	902	Elon Musk	400	2624	152.44

The third column shows the name of the wealthiest American at the start of that year. The fourth column shows his estimated wealth in billions of dollars. The numbers do seem to be trending upwards, but some of this is due to inflation. To remove that effect, we've converted their wealth to ounces of gold based on the price of gold at the time. The price of gold per ounce is shown in the fifth column. The last column shows his wealth in gold. The values in that column for the years 2000 and 2005 (210.53 and 108.14) are outliers because of a strong dollar and a weakening demand for gold during the Clinton years, as mentioned in a previous chapter. Those values aside, we see a definite upward trend in the real wealth of the richest American.

For example, Elon Musk in 2025 possessed 29 times as much wealth, in terms of gold, as the richest American in 1975, Daniel Ludwig. Looking at the names in the third column and considering the industries from which their wealth accrued (shipping, retail, television, personal computing, internet retail, online finance), it's apparent that the accumulation of wealth is facilitated by a technology-driven shrinking world. As transportation, communication, and information continue to be streamlined by advancing technology, the market for new products and services becomes global. Wealth explodes for those fortunate individuals who find themselves in the right place at the right time with the right ideas.

While this trend is surely welcomed by those who catch the express train to the top, one wonders if there may be an adverse effect on those left behind. In other words, in our Capitalist nation, is there such a thing as *too rich*? It's natural for some of us to envy those who have more than we have. But envy aside, does extreme wealth do non-monetary damage to those of us who are not so fortunate?

In the 2024 Election, Elon Musk spent more than a quarter of a billion dollars on the election campaign. On June 5, 2025, Musk wrote on his X platform (formerly Twitter), "Without me, Trump would have lost the election, Dems would control the House, and the Republicans would be 51-49 in the Senate." While the veracity of this statement can be debated, the notion that a single individual in a nation of more than 300 million could have such a profound effect is chilling. The premise of the

Founding Fathers is that people, not dollars, should have an equal voice.

Capitalism serves us well as the ideal economic system for a free society. Work hard. Work smart. Do what you're good at. Provide food, shelter, and clothing for you and your family. If you're ambitious and fortunate, you may accumulate extra wealth that allows you to purchase luxuries beyond the requirements of daily life. This is the *American Dream*, the rags-to-riches scenario, whereby freedom and capitalism can propel anyone who's willing to work smart and hard up the ladder of success. We are driven by the dual motivations of Capitalism: the desire to be rich, and the desire not to be poor.

At some point, however, one may become too rich. Excess wealth morphs from enabling the purchase of coveted luxuries to enabling the exercise of power. Money becomes a tool for control over others. At that point, the too-rich no longer view themselves as just another member of the group **We the People**. As kings of finance, they believe that they are best qualified to make decisions for us since they are clearly better than us.

Money is power, and power can be abused. Karl Marx and Friedrich Engels laid out their solution to this problem in their pamphlet *The Communist Manifesto*, published in 1848. Their simplistic communal answer was to share the wealth equally. In the style of Robin Hood, they would take from the rich and give to the poor. Unfortunately, Marx and Engels would not live long enough to witness their design being implemented. Had they lived another century, they would have seen that Communism fails wherever it's tried. Its fundamental flaw is that it ignores human nature. Workers want to choose their professions, and they want to be compensated fairly for their efforts. They don't want to be breaking their backs digging ditches, as others are watching them while sipping lemonade in lawn chairs. This is the reason Communist countries must lock their borders to keep their citizens in. Otherwise, the hard workers will flee, preferring a life of freedom to one of government-monitored servitude.

Communism is not the answer. The economic system of Capitalism reflects the soul of a free nation and is the natural byproduct of freedom. We shouldn't discard the game of Capitalism because of its fringe conditions, namely the misfortunes of the too-poor and the abuses by the too-rich. Instead, we must address these extremes. The many government- and charity-sponsored social programs are a good start at helping the too-poor.

But what about the too-rich?

A possible solution is to put a cap on wealth. Here's how it works. As a player in the game, if you reach the cap, congratulations! You've won at the game of Capitalism. It's time for you to step aside and enjoy your wealth. Allow others to take your place. While you may continue to play, you may not accumulate further wealth.

In other words, too much can be too much. But what is that amount, how would a wealth cap work, and why should this be a part of the Constitution?

Before answering these questions, let's take a moment to acknowledge the extreme nature of this proposal. Beyond laws that restrict lying, cheating, stealing, and otherwise playing the game unfairly, the limits of Capitalism have never been restricted. At a corporate level, anti-trust laws have attempted to regulate the growth and expansion of corporations that achieved or threatened to achieve monopolistic power over their marketplaces. But limits have never been placed on individuals.

This is new.

The reason it's necessary now is that today's global economy allows the creation of kings without votes or revolutions. The kings of industry are the simple result of cashflow. This proposed restriction must be part of the Constitution because the Constitution is the only law written from the bottom up, by the people, for the people. The super rich will never permit conventional laws that curtail their wealth. Any threat to that wealth will unleash their power in a blowback of monumental proportions. Brace yourselves.

What would be a reasonable wealth cap? We want a number so high that most Americans would never dream of reaching it. As such, they won't be discouraged from still trying to achieve the *American Dream.* At the same time, we want a number low enough that the amount required to mount a campaign that would influence the rest of us would cause an unacceptable depletion of their resources. For example, Musk's expenditure of a quarter of a billion dollars in 2024 did not make a ripple in his pond of $400 billion. So, $400 billion is too high.

Rather than spending time debating the ideal cap, we'll simply acknowledge that any number is arbitrary, so we'll pick a number that seems about right: $100 million. Here's our thinking. Most Americans – we're guessing 99% of them – would dance a jig at the opportunity to retire with $100 million in the bank. Thus, this cap does not extinguish the *American Dream.* On the other hand, converting that money to power in the form of persuading or dissuading people to your way of thinking would likely cost millions, which we think the holder of $100 million would be reluctant to pay out.

For those of you thinking, "Wait a minute! My wealth is approaching $100 million, and I want ***more***," bear in mind that your spouse can also accumulate $100 million. Thus, the total wealth cap for you and your spouse is $200 million.

If this number doesn't work out, it can be amended later, but let's go with it for now. Because of inflation, it's prudent to convert the dollars to ounces of gold, or to the Goldars we introduced in an earlier chapter. Since the Goldar for 2025 (the price of gold in dollars per ounce as of the start of 2025) is $2624, $100 million can be translated by division to 38,110 Goldars. For simplicity, let's call it 40,000 Goldars, which is $105 million. Close enough.

Here's how it works. Only individuals who believe their wealth at the end of the year will be at or above 40,000 Goldars need to concern themselves with paperwork. The rest of us have no obligation beyond our normal tax requirements, so we can continue to work towards the dream of reaching the wealth cap. The rich among us have an additional tax reporting requirement. They must list and value their assets as of year-end and compare the total amount to 40,000 Goldars, where the Goldar value is computed as of the same year-end. Any excess amount is subject to an 80% tax, payable to the U.S. Treasury by April 15 of the following year. These individuals are free to donate or transfer their assets elsewhere before year-end if they prefer not to pay taxes on the excess.

For example, they might choose to donate the excess to a hospital, or a library, or to give company shares to their employees. Or they can give the excess to their friends, children, and grandchildren. It's up to them. They earned the money. This is not a take-from-the-rich and give-to-the-poor wealth tax, where the wealthy are punished for working hard and the poor are rewarded for their misfortune. Let the successful citizens incinerate their excess wealth in a furnace if they choose. The point is not to have them share their wealth with those less fortunate but to ensure that they cannot use the power of excess wealth to control their fellow citizens.

Nor does the cap on wealth imply forced retirement. The wealthy may continue working. The only catch is that they must now give their excess wealth away.

Billionaires may understandably object to this proposal, arguing that they have rightly earned their riches, and have done so while following all rules and laws. However, that wealth accumulation was made possible largely because of the fertile American marketplace that the Constitution and government established specifically to protect those rules and laws. All we're suggesting here is that the time has come for the rules of the game to change. The unlimited accumulation of excess wealth is no longer deemed to be in the best interest of **We the People**.

To phase this in so that the effect is less traumatic for the super wealthy, the tax rate on the excess begins at 10% from the date of ratification of the new Constitution and increases by 10% each year up to the final rate of 80%. Here's the new wording in Article 4, Section 12:

> *To preclude abuse inherent in the power of excess wealth, citizens are limited to 40,000 Goldars of constructively owned assets, as determined at each year-end. Excess shall be taxed at 80% payable to the United States Treasury by the 15th day of April following the year-end. The exception is*

that from the seven years from year-end 20xx to year-end 20yy, the tax rate is the lesser of 80% or ten times (yyyy-20xx) where yyyy is the current year-end.

The term *constructively owned* implies that the citizen has control of that wealth, whether in his name or not. The intent is to dissuade citizens from hiding wealth, say in the name of friends or relatives. Fraud is punished by criminal and civil penalties as legislated by Congress. The term *citizens or residents* puts this tax burden on all those who are in line to benefit from life in the United States.

As mentioned above, those who are fortunate enough to reach the wealth cap are free to continue working and being productive members of society. The excess may be given away or passed on to Uncle Sam in the form of the taxes described. Or, for those who have come to love their wealth more than they love the country that makes such wealth possible, they are free to cling to their wealth by renouncing their citizenship and relocating to a foreign land.

Such expatriates would do well to consider that choice carefully. The American consumers who contributed to their wealth may have second thoughts about continuing to buy products and services from an expatriated foreigner. Also, the foreign country of choice may come to resent the power exercised by such billionaires on their politics. Consequently, they may tweak their own Constitutions to include a similar wealth cap.

Sovereign Immunity

The concept of immunity implies exemption from the rules. For example, *diplomatic immunity* means a diplomat cannot be charged or prosecuted for breaking laws in the country where the diplomat is stationed. *Sovereign immunity* means the king, or other sovereign, cannot be prosecuted for breaking laws in the sovereign's jurisdiction.

There are reasons for diplomatic immunity. If a diplomat were not immune from local laws, bad actors in the host nation could trump up charges against the diplomat and thereby hold him hostage. Without a guarantee of immunity, diplomats might be reluctant to accept posts in unstable nations.

The general rationalization for sovereign immunity is that the king can do no wrong since he serves by divine right. This means that only God can judge the king. Since the king possesses the power to make or remake laws, no higher power exists to find him guilty of breaking laws, at least not in this life. Also, from a practical perspective, the king is too important to be distracted by frivolous charges and lawsuits.

In the context of establishing a constitution that defines a framework in which the laws of a democratic republic are forged, the issue of immunity must be addressed. Who, if anyone, is immune from acts and laws of Congress?

If you scan the Constitution, you'll find the word *immunity* only once, in the first clause of Article IV, Section 2:

> *The Citizens of each State shall be entitled to all Privileges and Immunities of Citizens in the several States.*

This clause does not grant immunity. It merely states that if non-resident citizens travel through or reside in another State, they should not suffer discrimination. All citizens should be treated the same regardless of their state of origin.

The fact that the Constitution is mum on the issue of sovereign immunity has historically cleared the way for two schools of thought. In the first, sovereign immunity must play no role in the U.S. Government since it was not explicitly mentioned in the Constitution. In the second, since sovereign immunity is an accepted aspect of English common law, it must still apply, or the Constitution would have explicitly rejected it. This second view is that though there's no longer a king, the government, which is a substitute for the king, must still enjoy sovereign immunity.

When scholars debate sovereign immunity, the 11th Amendment is often brought up. Here it is:

> *Amendment XI (Ratified February 7, 1795):*
>
> *The Judicial power of the United States shall not be construed to extend to any suit in law or equity, commenced or prosecuted against one of the United States by Citizens of another State, or by Citizens or Subjects of any Foreign State.*

What does this amendment have to do with sovereign immunity? Some background is in order.

During the American Revolutionary War, many of the colonies racked up considerable debt because of their participation in the war effort. After the war, creditors came calling for repayment. The colonies (States now) were unable to pay and were being overwhelmed by lawsuits from the creditors. Creditors who were residents in the same State being sued were rebuffed by the State courts and had no further recourse. Nonresident creditors, however, took note of wording in the new Constitution:

Article III, Section 2:

The judicial Power shall extend ... to Controversies ... between a State and Citizens of another State ...

If State courts ruled against them, creditors could appeal to federal court. Indeed, such a case, *Chisholm v. George*, worked its way up to the Supreme Court in 1793. The Court ruled against the State of Georgia in a 4-to-1 decision. Given this decision, the States could see the writing on the wall. They would have to pay their out-of-state debts, which might bankrupt them. Their Congressional members proposed a Constitutional Amendment, shown above, which was quickly ratified in 1795 as the first amendment beyond the Bill of Rights. In the spirit of truth-in-advertising, perhaps the amendment should have read,

Amendment XI (Ratified February 7, 1795):

So States can avoid having to repay Revolutionary War debts, non-resident creditors must be satisfied with the decisions of State courts and cannot seek relief from Federal courts.

This amendment was successful at achieving its pragmatic purpose of allowing States to renege on war debts, but in the process nullified the reasonable wording in Article III, Section 2. Non-residents of a State could no longer seek redress in Federal court. Moreover, the Eleventh Amendment now stood as a beacon proclaiming a degree of sovereign immunity for States. The decisions by States and their agents, when convenient, were now immune from the law. For future fans of sovereign immunity, the Eleventh Amendment became the rallying point.

Another common justification for sovereign immunity was the Tenth Amendment,

> *Amendment X:*
>
> *The powers not delegated to the United States by the Constitution, nor prohibited by it to the States, are reserved to the States respectively, or to the people.*

Here, the amendment is intended to emphasize that the federal government is not all-powerful and does not possess the ability to grant freedom or rights, but only to restrict them within the narrow confines of the Constitution. Ironically, this Amendment, especially in conjunction with the Eleventh Amendment, has instead been construed to reinforce the concept of State sovereignty and State sovereign immunity.

Over the centuries, court cases have been argued based on the expectation of sovereign immunity or its lack. Arguments have been made that immunity does and should exist, while others have argued that it does not and should not. We need not recount the logic in these cases because we know with certainty the one thing that these historical debaters knew as well. If the Constitution had been explicit about sovereign immunity, there would be no need for disagreement. Fortunately, we can now rectify that shortcoming, and we shall.

But which way do we go? Immunity or not?

Let's approach this question with an example. Suppose an employee of a construction company is careless with a tool and accidentally causes harm to a coworker. Perhaps the coworker loses an eye. At the same time, let's imagine that a few miles away a suspected terrorist is being interrogated by an agent of the U.S. Government. The enthusiastic agent is careless and accidentally injures the suspect, causing him to lose an eye.

In each case, an argument can be made for criminal charges and civil damages. From the criminal perspective, not only might the individual who caused the injury be charged with inflicting bodily harm, but his management might be charged if complicit. Similarly, a civil suit might be brought against the individual, against management, and even against the company or government agency. The civil suit would seek damages, i.e. money, for medical expenses, pain and suffering, and loss of future income.

The question we need to address is whether the agent of the U.S. Government should be given a free pass based on sovereign immunity. The argument for immunity is that since the agent works for the government, and since you can't sue the King, then you shouldn't be allowed to sue his American replacement, i.e., the government, its agencies, or its agents.

However, if we look at the arguments given above for

sovereign immunity, they fizzle within a constitutionally driven democratic republic. The government does not serve by divine right, but by the rules of the Constitution, which is an extension of the will of the people. The higher power, namely the judicial branch, has been intentionally stitched into the Constitution with the precise function of judging lawful compliance. The other argument for immunity, that the Government and its agents are too important to be distracted by frivolous charges and lawsuits, has no basis in reason or practicality. This would be like arguing that a bank robber should not be prosecuted because the trial and incarceration might interfere with his day job. Instead of enticing politicians and government employees with immunity as a job benefit, we are better served by informing them that if their intentions tend toward wrongdoing, they need not apply, as criminal charges and lawsuits are not frivolous but shall apply to all.

In short, for a nation in which the book of rules begins with the phrase We the People, no one is above the law, whether they serve the government or not. If special circumstances exist in which agents of the law should not be liable for their actions, these cases for immunity can be carefully crafted into the wording of the law. For example, if government interrogators need the freedom to damage the eyeballs of suspected terrorists, that wording can be written into law. Likewise, regarding the possible need for immunity from *civil* liability, specific laws can be drawn up to provide such protection from civil suits. By permitting immunity only as part of the law-making process, the people are consenting through their representatives to immunity under narrow circumstances. A free pass from prosecution should be the exception, not the rule.

Here then are the revisions to the new Constitution to

deal with sovereign immunity.

The Eleventh Amendment is removed so that the intent of Article III, Section 2 is restored:

The judicial Power shall extend to all Cases, in Law and Equity, arising under this Constitution, the Laws of the United States, and Treaties made, or which shall be made, under their Authority; -- to all Cases affecting Ambassadors, other public Ministers and Consuls; -- to all Cases of admiralty and maritime Jurisdiction; -- to Controversies to which the United States shall be a Party; -- to Controversies between two or more States; -- ***between a State and Citizens of another State****, --between Citizens of different States, --between Citizens of the same State claiming Lands under Grants of different States,* ***and between a State, or the Citizens thereof, and foreign States, Citizens or Subjects****.*

A new paragraph is added after Article I, Section 7, 2nd clause (in which the process of turning a Bill into Law is described):

No State or Agency or Officer of the State or Federal Government is immune from liability for violating any Act of Congress, or any provision of this Constitution unless expressly stated therein.

Epilogue

In 1787, America's brightest statesmen gathered in Philadelphia to compose a document that would define the rules for governing a nation of free people. As a guide, these educated men looked back to past civilizations. But this American endeavor had no twin in history.

They were starting with a blank slate.

In this book, we have the audacity to suggest that the resulting Constitution, though holding its own for two and a half centuries, is flawed. Furthermore, we suggest patches for those flaws. It's natural for you, the reader, to reject these suggestions as radical, and to assert that the Constitution proposed in this book would not, could not, should not ever replace the existing document.

But remember, the purpose of this book is not to present a Constitution that can be voted on as an amendment. The required political correctness to achieve that aim would have crippled our ability to objectively assess and propose. This work is a literary and artistic exercise that is primarily intended to encourage thought. However, this book's hidden aim goes deeper than that. In reviewing the weaknesses of the original Constitution, we hope to pull back the curtain.

We live in trying times. As a species whose evolutionary success hinges on the twin pillars of community and cooperation, we find ourselves shouting political arguments across the dinner table. We are so angry with one another, we fail to ask ourselves how this came to be. Convinced that the *other* half of the country is ignorant, we overlook our own life experiences, in school, in church, and in the community. Most people we've come to know are not ignorant. More often, they are kind, pleasant, and intelligent.

If we could step outside ourselves for a moment and listen to our words, we'd realize the source of our hostility. The contempt we cast comes from our leaders, from their social media, and from their news-channel propaganda.

Our Constitution has holes. It always has. In the past, our leaders nevertheless upheld their oath to abide by its spirit. Now, the wizards and witches of Oz capitalize on these holes to seize power and hold it. They stand behind a curtain of the American flag, booming a broadcast that keeps us terrified and misdirected. "Hate one another! There are two sides! Pick your side and despise the other! Don't peek behind the curtain!"

But in our hearts, we know their arguments are contrived. We are not on two sides. We are one. And that one is We the People.

The problem we face has nothing to do with the words we shout across the dinner table. The problem is the source of those words. Pull back the curtain and you will find our leaders, all of them, cowering behind their megaphones. While they speak of two opposing sides, they are in fact complicit. They are as aware of the holes in the Constitution as we are but see no benefit in filling them. Our leaders in government and industry thrive on the status quo, having evolved to leverage the maximum benefit from it. Their fear is not of one another, but of us, the people, who would wrest control from them.

As with Dorothy in Oz, we have always had the power within ourselves to return home, to leave the corrupt land of deceitful wizards and witches, and to regain control of our lives.

We need only don our ruby slippers, head to the polls, click our heels twice, and vote out all the incumbents, *especially* those who profess to be on our side.

We the People deserve a fresh start.

Appendix A: Original Constitution

We the People of the United States, in Order to form a more perfect Union, establish Justice, insure domestic Tranquility, provide for the common defence, promote the general Welfare, and secure the Blessings of Liberty to ourselves and our Posterity, do ordain and establish this Constitution for the United States of America.

Article. I.

Section. 1.

All legislative Powers herein granted shall be vested in a Congress of the United States, which shall consist of a Senate and House of Representatives.

Section. 2.

The House of Representatives shall be composed of Members chosen every second Year by the People of the several States, and the Electors in each State shall have the Qualifications requisite for Electors of the most numerous Branch of the State Legislature.

No Person shall be a Representative who shall not have attained to the Age of twenty five Years, and been seven Years a Citizen of the United States, and who shall not, when elected, be an Inhabitant of that State in which he shall be chosen.

Representatives and direct Taxes shall be apportioned among the several States which may be included within this Union, according to their respective Numbers, which shall be determined by adding to the whole Number of free Persons, including those bound to Service for a Term of Years, and excluding Indians not taxed, three fifths of all other Persons. The actual Enumeration shall be made within three Years after the first Meeting of the Congress of the United States, and within every subsequent

Term of ten Years, in such Manner as they shall by Law direct. The Number of Representatives shall not exceed one for every thirty Thousand, but each State shall have at Least one Representative; and until such enumeration shall be made, the State of New Hampshire shall be entitled to chuse three, Massachusetts eight, Rhode-Island and Providence Plantations one, Connecticut five, New-York six, New Jersey four, Pennsylvania eight, Delaware one, Maryland six, Virginia ten, North Carolina five, South Carolina five, and Georgia three.

When vacancies happen in the Representation from any State, the Executive Authority thereof shall issue Writs of Election to fill such Vacancies.

The House of Representatives shall chuse their Speaker and other Officers; and shall have the sole Power of Impeachment.

Section. 3.

The Senate of the United States shall be composed of two Senators from each State, chosen by the Legislature thereof, for six Years; and each Senator shall have one Vote.

Immediately after they shall be assembled in Consequence of the first Election, they shall be divided as equally as may be into three Classes. The Seats of the Senators of the first Class shall be vacated at the Expiration of the second Year, of the second Class at the Expiration of the fourth Year, and of the third Class at the Expiration of the sixth Year, so that one third may be chosen every second Year; and if Vacancies happen by Resignation, or otherwise, during the Recess of the Legislature of any State, the Executive thereof may make temporary Appointments until the next Meeting of the Legislature, which shall then fill such Vacancies.

No Person shall be a Senator who shall not have attained to the Age of thirty Years, and been nine Years a Citizen of the United States, and who shall not, when elected, be an Inhabitant of that State for which he shall be chosen.

The Vice President of the United States shall be President of the Senate, but shall have no Vote, unless they be equally divided.

The Senate shall chuse their other Officers, and also a President pro tempore, in the Absence of the Vice President, or when he shall exercise the Office of President of the United States.

The Senate shall have the sole Power to try all Impeachments. When sitting for that Purpose, they shall be on Oath or Affirmation. When the President of the United States is tried, the Chief Justice shall preside: And no Person shall be convicted without the Concurrence of two thirds of the Members present.

Judgment in Cases of Impeachment shall not extend further than to removal from Office, and disqualification to hold and enjoy any Office of honor, Trust or Profit under the United States: but the Party convicted shall nevertheless be liable and subject to Indictment, Trial, Judgment and Punishment, according to Law.

Section. 4.

The Times, Places and Manner of holding Elections for Senators and Representatives, shall be prescribed in each State by the Legislature thereof; but the Congress may at any time by Law make or alter such Regulations, except as to the Places of chusing Senators.

The Congress shall assemble at least once in every Year, and such Meeting shall be on the first Monday in December, unless they shall by Law appoint a different Day.

Section. 5.

Each House shall be the Judge of the Elections, Returns and Qualifications of its own Members, and a Majority of each shall constitute a Quorum to do Business; but a smaller Number may adjourn from day to day, and may be authorized to compel the Attendance of absent Members, in such Manner, and under such Penalties as each House may provide.

Each House may determine the Rules of its Proceedings, punish its Members for disorderly Behaviour, and, with the Concurrence of two thirds, expel a Member.

Each House shall keep a Journal of its Proceedings, and from time to time publish the same, excepting such Parts as may in their Judgment require Secrecy; and the Yeas and Nays of the Members of either House on any question shall, at the Desire of one fifth of those Present, be entered on the Journal.

Neither House, during the Session of Congress, shall, without the Consent of the other, adjourn for more than three days, nor to any other Place than that in which the two Houses shall be sitting.

Section. 6.

The Senators and Representatives shall receive a Compensation for their Services, to be ascertained by Law, and paid out of the Treasury of the United States. They shall in all Cases, except Treason, Felony and Breach of the Peace, be privileged from Arrest during their Attendance at the Session of their respective Houses, and in going to and returning from the same; and for any Speech or Debate in either House, they shall not be questioned in any other Place.

No Senator or Representative shall, during the Time for which he was elected, be appointed to any civil Office under the Authority of the United States, which shall have been created, or the Emoluments whereof shall have been encreased during such time; and no Person holding any Office under the United States, shall be a Member of either House during his Continuance in Office.

Section. 7.

All Bills for raising Revenue shall originate in the House of Representatives; but the Senate may propose or concur with Amendments as on other Bills.

Every Bill which shall have passed the House of Representatives and the Senate, shall, before it become a Law, be presented to the President of the United States; If he approve he shall sign it, but if not he shall return it, with his Objections to that House in which it shall have originated, who shall enter the Objections at large on their Journal, and proceed to reconsider it. If after such Reconsideration two thirds of that House shall agree to pass the Bill, it shall be sent, together with the Objections, to the other House, by which it shall likewise be reconsidered, and if approved by two thirds of that House, it shall become a Law. But in all such Cases the Votes of both Houses shall be determined by yeas and Nays, and the Names of the Persons voting for and against the Bill shall be entered on the Journal of each House respectively. If any Bill shall not be returned by the President within ten Days (Sundays excepted) after it shall have been presented to him, the Same shall be a Law, in like Manner as if he had signed it, unless the Congress by their Adjournment prevent its Return, in which Case it shall not be a Law.

Every Order, Resolution, or Vote to which the Concurrence of the Senate and House of Representatives may be necessary (except on a question of Adjournment) shall be presented to the President of the United States; and before the Same shall take Effect, shall be approved by him, or being disapproved by him, shall be repassed by two thirds of the Senate and House of Representatives, according to the Rules and Limitations prescribed in the Case of a Bill.

Section. 8.

The Congress shall have Power To lay and collect Taxes, Duties, Imposts and Excises, to pay the Debts and provide for the common Defence and general Welfare of the United States; but all Duties, Imposts and Excises shall be uniform throughout the United States;

To borrow Money on the credit of the United States;

To regulate Commerce with foreign Nations, and among the several States, and with the Indian Tribes;

To establish an uniform Rule of Naturalization, and uniform Laws on the subject of Bankruptcies throughout the United States;

To coin Money, regulate the Value thereof, and of foreign Coin, and fix the Standard of Weights and Measures;

To provide for the Punishment of counterfeiting the Securities and current Coin of the United States;

To establish Post Offices and post Roads;

To promote the Progress of Science and useful Arts, by securing for limited Times to Authors and Inventors the exclusive Right to their respective Writings and Discoveries;

To constitute Tribunals inferior to the supreme Court;

To define and punish Piracies and Felonies committed on the high Seas, and Offences against the Law of Nations;

To declare War, grant Letters of Marque and Reprisal, and make Rules concerning Captures on Land and Water;

To raise and support Armies, but no Appropriation of Money to that Use shall be for a longer Term than two Years;

To provide and maintain a Navy;

To make Rules for the Government and Regulation of the land and naval Forces;

To provide for calling forth the Militia to execute the Laws of the Union, suppress Insurrections and repel Invasions;

To provide for organizing, arming, and disciplining, the Militia, and for governing such Part of them as may be employed in the Service of the United States, reserving to the States respectively, the Appointment of the Officers, and the Authority of training the Militia according to the discipline prescribed by Congress;

To exercise exclusive Legislation in all Cases whatsoever, over such District (not exceeding ten Miles square) as may, by Cession of particular States, and the Acceptance of Congress, become the Seat of the Government of the United States, and to exercise like Authority over all Places purchased by the Consent of the Legislature of the State in which the Same shall be, for the Erection of Forts, Magazines, Arsenals, dock-Yards, and other needful Buildings; --And

To make all Laws which shall be necessary and proper for carrying into Execution the foregoing Powers, and all other Powers vested by this Constitution in the Government of the United States, or in any Department or Officer thereof.

Section. 9.

The Migration or Importation of such Persons as any of the States now existing shall think proper to admit, shall not be prohibited by the Congress prior to the Year one thousand eight hundred and eight, but a Tax or duty may be imposed on such

Importation, not exceeding ten dollars for each Person.

The Privilege of the Writ of Habeas Corpus shall not be suspended, unless when in Cases of Rebellion or Invasion the public Safety may require it.

No Bill of Attainder or ex post facto Law shall be passed.

No Capitation, or other direct, Tax shall be laid, unless in Proportion to the Census or enumeration herein before directed to be taken.

No Tax or Duty shall be laid on Articles exported from any State.

No Preference shall be given by any Regulation of Commerce or Revenue to the Ports of one State over those of another: nor shall Vessels bound to, or from, one State, be obliged to enter, clear, or pay Duties in another.

No Money shall be drawn from the Treasury, but in Consequence of Appropriations made by Law; and a regular Statement and Account of the Receipts and Expenditures of all public Money shall be published from time to time.

No Title of Nobility shall be granted by the United States: And no Person holding any Office of Profit or Trust under them, shall, without the Consent of the Congress, accept of any present, Emolument, Office, or Title, of any kind whatever, from any King, Prince, or foreign State.

Section. 10.

No State shall enter into any Treaty, Alliance, or Confederation; grant Letters of Marque and Reprisal; coin Money; emit Bills of Credit; make any Thing but gold and silver Coin a Tender in Payment of Debts; pass any Bill of Attainder, ex post facto Law, or Law impairing the Obligation of Contracts, or grant any Title of Nobility.

No State shall, without the Consent of the Congress, lay any Imposts or Duties on Imports or Exports, except what may be absolutely necessary for executing it's inspection Laws: and the net Produce of all Duties and Imposts, laid by any State on Imports or Exports, shall be for the Use of the Treasury of the United States; and all such Laws shall be subject to the Revision and Controul of the Congress.

No State shall, without the Consent of Congress, lay any Duty of Tonnage, keep Troops, or Ships of War in time of Peace, enter into any Agreement or Compact with another State, or with a foreign Power, or engage in War, unless actually invaded, or in such imminent Danger as will not admit of delay.

Article. II.

Section. 1.

The executive Power shall be vested in a President of the United States of America. He shall hold his Office during the Term of four Years, and, together with the Vice President, chosen for the same Term, be elected, as follows

Each State shall appoint, in such Manner as the Legislature thereof may direct, a Number of Electors, equal to the whole Number of Senators and Representatives to which the State may be entitled in the Congress: but no Senator or Representative, or Person holding an Office of Trust or Profit under the United States, shall be appointed an Elector.

The Electors shall meet in their respective States, and vote by Ballot for two Persons, of whom one at least shall not be an Inhabitant of the same State with themselves. And they shall make a List of all the Persons voted for, and of the Number of Votes for each; which List they shall sign and certify, and transmit sealed to the Seat of the Government of the United States, directed to the President of the Senate. The President of the Senate shall, in the Presence of the Senate and House of Representatives, open all the Certificates, and the Votes shall then be counted. The Person having the greatest Number of Votes shall be the President, if such Number be a Majority of the whole Number of Electors appointed; and if there be more than one who have such Majority, and have an equal Number of Votes, then the House of Representatives shall immediately chuse by Ballot one of them for President; and if no Person have a Majority, then from the five highest on the List the said House shall in like Manner chuse the President. But in chusing the President, the Votes shall be taken by States, the Representation from each State having one Vote; A quorum for this Purpose shall consist of a Member or

Members from two thirds of the States, and a Majority of all the States shall be necessary to a Choice. In every Case, after the Choice of the President, the Person having the greatest Number of Votes of the Electors shall be the Vice President. But if there should remain two or more who have equal Votes, the Senate shall chuse from them by Ballot the Vice President.

The Congress may determine the Time of chusing the Electors, and the Day on which they shall give their Votes; which Day shall be the same throughout the United States.

No Person except a natural born Citizen, or a Citizen of the United States, at the time of the Adoption of this Constitution, shall be eligible to the Office of President; neither shall any Person be eligible to that Office who shall not have attained to the Age of thirty five Years, and been fourteen Years a Resident within the United States.

In Case of the Removal of the President from Office, or of his Death, Resignation, or Inability to discharge the Powers and Duties of the said Office, the Same shall devolve on the Vice President, and the Congress may by Law provide for the Case of Removal, Death, Resignation or Inability, both of the President and Vice President, declaring what Officer shall then act as President, and such Officer shall act accordingly, until the Disability be removed, or a President shall be elected.

The President shall, at stated Times, receive for his Services, a Compensation, which shall neither be encreased nor diminished during the Period for which he shall have been elected, and he shall not receive within that Period any other Emolument from the United States, or any of them.

Before he enter on the Execution of his Office, he shall take the following Oath or Affirmation: --"I do solemnly swear (or affirm) that I will faithfully execute the Office of President of the United States, and will to the best of my Ability, preserve, protect and defend the Constitution of the United States."

Section. 2.

The President shall be Commander in Chief of the Army and Navy of the United States, and of the Militia of the several States, when called into the actual Service of the United States;

he may require the Opinion, in writing, of the principal Officer in each of the executive Departments, upon any Subject relating to the Duties of their respective Offices, and he shall have Power to grant Reprieves and Pardons for Offences against the United States, except in Cases of Impeachment.

He shall have Power, by and with the Advice and Consent of the Senate, to make Treaties, provided two thirds of the Senators present concur; and he shall nominate, and by and with the Advice and Consent of the Senate, shall appoint Ambassadors, other public Ministers and Consuls, Judges of the supreme Court, and all other Officers of the United States, whose Appointments are not herein otherwise provided for, and which shall be established by Law: but the Congress may by Law vest the Appointment of such inferior Officers, as they think proper, in the President alone, in the Courts of Law, or in the Heads of Departments.

The President shall have Power to fill up all Vacancies that may happen during the Recess of the Senate, by granting Commissions which shall expire at the End of their next Session.

Section. 3.

He shall from time to time give to the Congress Information of the State of the Union, and recommend to their Consideration such Measures as he shall judge necessary and expedient; he may, on extraordinary Occasions, convene both Houses, or either of them, and in Case of Disagreement between them, with Respect to the Time of Adjournment, he may adjourn them to such Time as he shall think proper; he shall receive Ambassadors and other public Ministers; he shall take Care that the Laws be faithfully executed, and shall Commission all the Officers of the United States.

Section. 4.

The President, Vice President and all civil Officers of the United States, shall be removed from Office on Impeachment for, and Conviction of, Treason, Bribery, or other high Crimes and Misdemeanors.

Article. III.

Section. 1.

The judicial Power of the United States, shall be vested in one supreme Court, and in such inferior Courts as the Congress may from time to time ordain and establish. The Judges, both of the supreme and inferior Courts, shall hold their Offices during good Behaviour, and shall, at stated Times, receive for their Services, a Compensation, which shall not be diminished during their Continuance in Office.

Section. 2.

The judicial Power shall extend to all Cases, in Law and Equity, arising under this Constitution, the Laws of the United States, and Treaties made, or which shall be made, under their Authority; --to all Cases affecting Ambassadors, other public Ministers and Consuls; --to all Cases of admiralty and maritime Jurisdiction; --to Controversies to which the United States shall be a Party; --to Controversies between two or more States; --between a State and Citizens of another State, --between Citizens of different States, --between Citizens of the same State claiming Lands under Grants of different States, and between a State, or the Citizens thereof, and foreign States, Citizens or Subjects.

In all Cases affecting Ambassadors, other public Ministers and Consuls, and those in which a State shall be Party, the supreme Court shall have original Jurisdiction. In all the other Cases before mentioned, the supreme Court shall have appellate Jurisdiction, both as to Law and Fact, with such Exceptions, and under such Regulations as the Congress shall make.

The Trial of all Crimes, except in Cases of Impeachment, shall be by Jury; and such Trial shall be held in the State where the said Crimes shall have been committed; but when not committed within any State, the Trial shall be at such Place or Places as the Congress may by Law have directed.

Section. 3.

Treason against the United States, shall consist only in levying War against them, or in adhering to their Enemies, giving them Aid and Comfort. No Person shall be convicted of Treason unless on the Testimony of two Witnesses to the same overt Act, or on Confession in open Court.

The Congress shall have Power to declare the Punishment of Treason, but no Attainder of Treason shall work Corruption of Blood, or Forfeiture except during the Life of the Person attainted.

Article. IV.

Section. 1.

Full Faith and Credit shall be given in each State to the public Acts, Records, and judicial Proceedings of every other State. And the Congress may by general Laws prescribe the Manner in which such Acts, Records and Proceedings shall be proved, and the Effect thereof.

Section. 2.

The Citizens of each State shall be entitled to all Privileges and Immunities of Citizens in the several States.

A Person charged in any State with Treason, Felony, or other Crime, who shall flee from Justice, and be found in another State, shall on Demand of the executive Authority of the State from which he fled, be delivered up, to be removed to the State having Jurisdiction of the Crime.

No Person held to Service or Labour in one State, under the Laws thereof, escaping into another, shall, in Consequence of any Law or Regulation therein, be discharged from such Service or Labour, but shall be delivered up on Claim of the Party to whom such Service or Labour may be due.

Section. 3.

New States may be admitted by the Congress into this Union; but no new State shall be formed or erected within the Jurisdiction of any other State; nor any State be formed by the Junction of two or more States, or Parts of States, without the Consent of the Legislatures of the States concerned as well as of the Congress.

The Congress shall have Power to dispose of and make all needful Rules and Regulations respecting the Territory or other Property belonging to the United States; and nothing in this Constitution shall be so construed as to Prejudice any Claims of the United States, or of any particular State.

Section. 4.

The United States shall guarantee to every State in this Union a Republican Form of Government, and shall protect each of them against Invasion; and on Application of the Legislature, or of the Executive (when the Legislature cannot be convened) against domestic Violence.

Article. V.

The Congress, whenever two thirds of both Houses shall deem it necessary, shall propose Amendments to this Constitution, or, on the Application of the Legislatures of two thirds of the several States, shall call a Convention for proposing Amendments, which, in either Case, shall be valid to all Intents and Purposes, as Part of this Constitution, when ratified by the Legislatures of three fourths of the several States, or by Conventions in three fourths thereof, as the one or the other Mode of Ratification may be proposed by the Congress; Provided that no Amendment which may be made prior to the Year One thousand eight hundred and eight shall in any Manner affect the first and fourth Clauses in the Ninth Section of the first Article; and that no State, without its Consent, shall be deprived of its equal Suffrage in the Senate.

Article. VI.

All Debts contracted and Engagements entered into, before the Adoption of this Constitution, shall be as valid against the United States under this Constitution, as under the Confederation.

This Constitution, and the Laws of the United States which shall be made in Pursuance thereof; and all Treaties made, or which shall be made, under the Authority of the United States, shall be the supreme Law of the Land; and the Judges in every State shall be bound thereby, any Thing in the Constitution or Laws of any State to the Contrary notwithstanding.

The Senators and Representatives before mentioned, and the Members of the several State Legislatures, and all executive and judicial Officers, both of the United States and of the several States, shall be bound by Oath or Affirmation, to support this Constitution; but no religious Test shall ever be required as a Qualification to any Office or public Trust under the United States.

Article. VII.

The Ratification of the Conventions of nine States, shall be sufficient for the Establishment of this Constitution between the States so ratifying the Same.

The Word, "the," being interlined between the seventh and eighth Lines of the first Page, The Word "Thirty" being partly written on an Erazure in the fifteenth Line of the first Page, The Words "is tried" being interlined between the thirty second and thirty third Lines of the first Page and the Word "the" being interlined between the forty third and forty fourth Lines of the second Page.

Attest William Jackson Secretary

done in Convention by the Unanimous Consent of the States present the Seventeenth Day of September in the Year of our

Lord one thousand seven hundred and Eighty seven and of the Independance of the United States of America the Twelfth In witness whereof We have hereunto subscribed our Names,

(signatures follow).

Amendment I

Congress shall make no law respecting an establishment of religion, or prohibiting the free exercise thereof; or abridging the freedom of speech, or of the press; or the right of the people peaceably to assemble, and to petition the Government for a redress of grievances.

Amendment II

A well regulated Militia, being necessary to the security of a free State, the right of the people to keep and bear Arms, shall not be infringed.

Amendment III

No Soldier shall, in time of peace be quartered in any house, without the consent of the Owner, nor in time of war, but in a manner to be prescribed by law.

Amendment IV

The right of the people to be secure in their persons, houses, papers, and effects, against unreasonable searches and seizures, shall not be violated, and no Warrants shall issue, but upon probable cause, supported by Oath or affirmation, and particularly describing the place to be searched, and the persons or things to be seized.

Amendment V

No person shall be held to answer for a capital, or otherwise infamous crime, unless on a presentment or indictment of a Grand Jury, except in cases arising in the land or naval forces, or in the Militia, when in actual service in time of War or public danger; nor shall any person be subject for the same offence to be twice put in jeopardy of life or limb; nor shall be compelled in any criminal case to be a witness against himself, nor be deprived of life, liberty, or property, without due process of law; nor shall private property be taken for public use, without just compensation.

Amendment VI

In all criminal prosecutions, the accused shall enjoy the right to a speedy and public trial, by an impartial jury of the State and district wherein the crime shall have been committed, which district shall have been previously ascertained by law, and to be informed of the nature and cause of the accusation; to be confronted with the witnesses against him; to have compulsory process for obtaining witnesses in his favor, and to have the Assistance of Counsel for his defence.

Amendment VII

In Suits at common law, where the value in controversy shall exceed twenty dollars, the right of trial by jury shall be preserved, and no fact tried by a jury, shall be otherwise reexamined in any Court of the United States, than according to the rules of the common law.

Amendment VIII

Excessive bail shall not be required, nor excessive fines imposed, nor cruel and unusual punishments inflicted.

Amendment IX

The enumeration in the Constitution, of certain rights, shall not be construed to deny or disparage others retained by the people.

Amendment X

The powers not delegated to the United States by the Constitution, nor prohibited by it to the States, are reserved to the States respectively, or to the people.

Amendment XI

The Judicial power of the United States shall not be construed to extend to any suit in law or equity, commenced or prosecuted against one of the United States by Citizens of another State, or by Citizens or Subjects of any Foreign State.

Amendment XII

The Electors shall meet in their respective states and vote by ballot for President and Vice-President, one of whom, at least, shall not be an inhabitant of the same state with themselves; they shall name in their ballots the person voted for as President, and in distinct ballots the person voted for as Vice-President, and they shall make distinct lists of all persons voted for as President, and of all persons voted for as Vice-President, and of the number of votes for each, which lists they shall sign and certify, and transmit sealed to the seat of the government of the United States, directed to the President of the Senate; -- the President of the Senate shall, in the presence of the Senate and House of Representatives, open all the certificates and the votes shall then be counted; -- The person having the greatest number of votes for President, shall be the President, if such number be a majority of the whole number of Electors appointed; and if no person have such majority, then from the persons having the highest numbers not exceeding three on the list of those voted for as President, the House of Representatives shall choose immediately, by ballot, the President. But in choosing the President, the votes shall be taken by states, the representation from each state having one vote; a quorum for this purpose shall consist of a member or members from two-thirds of the states, and a majority of all the states shall be necessary to a choice. And if the House of Representatives shall not choose a President whenever the right of choice shall devolve upon them, before the fourth day of March next following, then the Vice-President shall act as President, as in case of the death or other constitutional disability of the President. The person having the greatest number of votes as Vice-President, shall be the Vice-President, if such number be a majority of the whole number of Electors appointed, and if no person have a majority, then from the two highest numbers on the list, the Senate shall choose the Vice-President; a quorum for the purpose shall consist of two-thirds of the whole number of Senators, and a majority of the whole number shall be necessary to a choice. But no person constitutionally ineligible to the office of President shall be eligible to that of Vice-President of the United States.

Amendment XIII

Section 1.

Neither slavery nor involuntary servitude, except as a punishment for crime whereof the party shall have been duly convicted, shall exist within the United States, or any place subject to their jurisdiction.

Section 2.

Congress shall have power to enforce this article by appropriate legislation.

Amendment XIV

Section 1.

All persons born or naturalized in the United States, and subject to the jurisdiction thereof, are citizens of the United States and of the State wherein they reside. No State shall make or enforce any law which shall abridge the privileges or immunities of citizens of the United States; nor shall any State deprive any person of life, liberty, or property, without due process of law; nor deny to any person within its jurisdiction the equal protection of the laws.

Section 2.

Representatives shall be apportioned among the several States according to their respective numbers, counting the whole number of persons in each State, excluding Indians not taxed. But when the right to vote at any election for the choice of electors for President and Vice-President of the United States, Representatives in Congress, the Executive and Judicial officers of a State, or the members of the Legislature thereof, is denied to any of the male inhabitants of such State, being twenty-one years of age, and citizens of the United States, or in any way abridged, except for participation in rebellion, or other crime, the basis of representation therein shall be reduced in the proportion which the number of such male citizens shall bear to the whole number of male citizens twenty-one years of age in such State.

Section 3.

No person shall be a Senator or Representative in Congress, or elector of President and Vice-President, or hold any office, civil or military, under the United States, or under any State, who, having previously taken an oath, as a member of Congress, or as an officer of the United States, or as a member of any State legislature, or as an executive or judicial officer of any State, to support the Constitution of the United States, shall have engaged in insurrection or rebellion against the same, or given aid or comfort to the enemies thereof. But Congress may by a vote of two-thirds of each House, remove such disability.

Section 4.

The validity of the public debt of the United States, authorized by law, including debts incurred for payment of pensions and bounties for services in suppressing insurrection or rebellion, shall not be questioned. But neither the United States nor any State shall assume or pay any debt or obligation incurred in aid of insurrection or rebellion against the United States, or any claim for the loss or emancipation of any slave; but all such debts, obligations and claims shall be held illegal and void.

Section 5.

The Congress shall have power to enforce, by appropriate legislation, the provisions of this article.

Amendment XV

Section 1.

The right of citizens of the United States to vote shall not be denied or abridged by the United States or by any State on account of race, color, or previous condition of servitude--

Section 2.

The Congress shall have power to enforce this article by appropriate legislation.

Amendment XVI

The Congress shall have power to lay and collect taxes on

incomes, from whatever source derived, without apportionment among the several States, and without regard to any census or enumeration.

Amendment XVII

The Senate of the United States shall be composed of two Senators from each State, elected by the people thereof, for six years; and each Senator shall have one vote. The electors in each State shall have the qualifications requisite for electors of the most numerous branch of the State legislatures.

When vacancies happen in the representation of any State in the Senate, the executive authority of such State shall issue writs of election to fill such vacancies: Provided, That the legislature of any State may empower the executive thereof to make temporary appointments until the people fill the vacancies by election as the legislature may direct.

This amendment shall not be so construed as to affect the election or term of any Senator chosen before it becomes valid as part of the Constitution.

Amendment XVIII

Section 1.

After one year from the ratification of this article the manufacture, sale, or transportation of intoxicating liquors within, the importation thereof into, or the exportation thereof from the United States and all territory subject to the jurisdiction thereof for beverage purposes is hereby prohibited.

Section 2.

The Congress and the several States shall have concurrent power to enforce this article by appropriate legislation.

Section 3.

This article shall be inoperative unless it shall have been ratified as an amendment to the Constitution by the legislatures of the several States, as provided in the Constitution, within seven years from the date of the submission hereof to the States by the Congress.

Amendment XIX

The right of citizens of the United States to vote shall not be denied or abridged by the United States or by any State on account of sex.

Congress shall have power to enforce this article by appropriate legislation.

Amendment XX

Section 1.

The terms of the President and the Vice President shall end at noon on the 20th day of January, and the terms of Senators and Representatives at noon on the 3d day of January, of the years in which such terms would have ended if this article had not been ratified; and the terms of their successors shall then begin.

Section 2.

The Congress shall assemble at least once in every year, and such meeting shall begin at noon on the 3d day of January, unless they shall by law appoint a different day.

Section 3.

If, at the time fixed for the beginning of the term of the President, the President elect shall have died, the Vice President elect shall become President. If a President shall not have been chosen before the time fixed for the beginning of his term, or if the President elect shall have failed to qualify, then the Vice President elect shall act as President until a President shall have qualified; and the Congress may by law provide for the case wherein neither a President elect nor a Vice President elect shall have qualified, declaring who shall then act as President, or the manner in which one who is to act shall be selected, and such person shall act accordingly until a President or Vice President shall have qualified.

Section 4.

The Congress may by law provide for the case of the death of any of the persons from whom the House of Representatives may choose a President whenever the right of choice shall have devolved upon them, and for the case of the death of any of the persons from whom the Senate may choose a Vice President whenever the right of choice shall have devolved upon them.

Section 5.

Sections 1 and 2 shall take effect on the 15th day of October following the ratification of this article.

Section 6.

This article shall be inoperative unless it shall have been ratified as an amendment to the Constitution by the legislatures of three-fourths of the several States within seven years from the date of its submission.

Amendment XXI

Section 1.

The eighteenth article of amendment to the Constitution of the United States is hereby repealed.

Section 2.

The transportation or importation into any State, Territory, or possession of the United States for delivery or use therein of intoxicating liquors, in violation of the laws thereof, is hereby prohibited.

Section 3.

This article shall be inoperative unless it shall have been ratified as an amendment to the Constitution by conventions in the several States, as provided in the Constitution, within seven years from the date of the submission hereof to the States by the Congress.

Amendment XXII

Section 1.

No person shall be elected to the office of the President more than twice, and no person who has held the office of President, or acted as President, for more than two years of a term to which some other person was elected President shall be elected to the office of the President more than once. But this Article shall not apply to any person holding the office of President when this Article was proposed by the Congress, and shall not prevent any person who may be holding the office of President, or acting as President, during the term within which this Article becomes operative from holding the office of President or acting as President during the remainder of such term.

Section 2.

This article shall be inoperative unless it shall have been ratified as an amendment to the Constitution by the legislatures of three-fourths of the several States within seven years from the date of its submission to the States by the Congress.

Amendment XXIII

Section 1.

The District constituting the seat of Government of the United States shall appoint in such manner as the Congress may direct:

A number of electors of President and Vice President equal to the whole number of Senators and Representatives in Congress to which the District would be entitled if it were a State, but in no event more than the least populous State; they shall be in addition to those appointed by the States, but they shall be considered, for the purposes of the election of President and Vice President, to be electors appointed by a State; and they shall meet in the District and perform such duties as provided by the twelfth article of amendment.

Section 2.

The Congress shall have power to enforce this article by appropriate legislation.

Amendment XXIV

Section 1.

The right of citizens of the United States to vote in any primary or other election for President or Vice President, for electors for President or Vice President, or for Senator or Representative in Congress, shall not be denied or abridged by the United States or any State by reason of failure to pay any poll tax or other tax.

Section 2.

The Congress shall have power to enforce this article by appropriate legislation.

Amendment XXV

Section 1.

In case of the removal of the President from office or of his death or resignation, the Vice President shall become President.

Section 2.

Whenever there is a vacancy in the office of the Vice President, the President shall nominate a Vice President who shall take office upon confirmation by a majority vote of both Houses of Congress.

Section 3.

Whenever the President transmits to the President pro tempore of the Senate and the Speaker of the House of Representatives his written declaration that he is unable to discharge the powers and duties of his office, and until he transmits to them a written declaration to the contrary, such powers and duties shall be discharged by the Vice President as Acting President.

Section 4.

Whenever the Vice President and a majority of either the principal officers of the executive departments or of such other body as Congress may by law provide, transmit to the President pro tempore of the Senate and the Speaker of the House of Representatives their written declaration that the President is unable to discharge the powers and duties of his office, the Vice President shall immediately assume the powers and duties of the office as Acting President.

Thereafter, when the President transmits to the President pro tempore of the Senate and the Speaker of the House of Representatives his written declaration that no inability exists, he shall resume the powers and duties of his office unless the Vice President and a majority of either the principal officers of the executive department or of such other body as Congress may by law provide, transmit within four days to the President pro tempore of the Senate and the Speaker of the House of Representatives their written declaration that the President is unable to discharge the powers and duties of his office. Thereupon Congress shall decide the issue, assembling within forty-eight hours for that purpose if not in session. If the Congress, within twenty-one days after receipt of the latter written declaration, or, if Congress is not in session, within twenty-one days after Congress is required to assemble, determines by two-thirds vote of both Houses that the President is unable to discharge the powers and duties of his office, the Vice President shall continue to discharge the same as Acting President; otherwise, the President shall resume the powers and duties of his office.

Amendment XXVI

Section 1.

The right of citizens of the United States, who are eighteen years of age or older, to vote shall not be denied or abridged by the United States or by any State on account of age.

Section 2.

The Congress shall have power to enforce this article by appropriate legislation.

Amendment XXVII

No law, varying the compensation for the services of the Senators and Representatives, shall take effect, until an election of Representatives shall have intervened.

Appendix B: Current Constitution

We the People of the United States, in Order to form a more perfect Union, establish Justice, **insure** domestic Tranquility, provide for the common **defence**, promote the general Welfare, and secure the Blessings of Liberty to ourselves and our Posterity, do ordain and establish this Constitution for the United States of America.

Article I.

Section 1.

All legislative Powers herein granted shall be vested in a Congress of the United States, which shall consist of a Senate and House of Representatives.

Section 2.

The House of Representatives shall be composed of Members chosen every second Year by the People of the several States, **and the Electors in each State shall have the Qualifications requisite for Electors of the most numerous Branch of the State Legislature.**

No Person shall be a Representative who shall not have attained to the Age of twenty-five Years, and been seven Years a Citizen of the United States, and who shall not, when elected, be an Inhabitant of that State in which he shall be chosen.

Representatives shall be apportioned among the several States which may be included within this Union, according to

Appendix C: New Constitution

We the People of the United States, in Order to form a more perfect Union, establish Justice, **ensure** domestic Tranquility, provide for the common **defense**, promote the general Welfare, and secure the Blessings of Liberty to ourselves and our Posterity, do ordain and establish this Constitution for the United States of America.

Article I. Congress – The Legislative Branch

Section 1. Overview

All legislative Powers herein granted shall be vested in a Congress of the United States, which shall consist of a Senate and House of Representatives.

Section 2. The House of Representatives

The House of Representatives shall be composed of Members chosen every second Year by the People of the several States.

No Person shall be a Representative who shall not have attained to the Age of twenty-five Years, and been seven Years a Citizen of the United States, and who shall not, when elected, be an Inhabitant of that State in which he shall be chosen; **neither shall any Person be eligible to that Office who has been elected to that Office more than three times, or has been elected to that Office three times and held the office of Representative, or acted as Representative, for more than one year of a term to which some other person was elected Representative.**

Representatives shall be apportioned among the several States which may be included within this Union, according to their respective Numbers, which shall be determined as the whole number of persons in each State, **excluding Indians not taxed. But when the right to vote at any election for the choice of electors for President and Vice-President of the United States, Representatives in Congress, the Executive and Judicial officers of a State, or the members of the Legislature thereof, is denied to any of the male inhabitants of such State, being eighteen years of age, and citizens of the United States, or in any way abridged, except for participation in rebellion, or other crime, the basis of representation therein shall be reduced in the proportion which the number of such male citizens shall bear to the whole number of male citizens eighteen years of age in such State.**

The actual Enumeration shall be made **within three Years after the first Meeting of the Congress of the United States, and within every subsequent Term of ten Years, in such Manner as they shall by Law direct. The Number of Representatives shall not exceed one for every thirty Thousand, but each State shall have at Least one Representative; and until such enumeration shall be made, the State of New Hampshire shall be entitled to chuse three, Massachusetts eight, Rhode-Island and Providence Plantations one, Connecticut five, New-York six, New Jersey four, Pennsylvania eight, Delaware one, Maryland six, Virginia ten, North Carolina five, South Carolina five, and Georgia three.**

their respective Numbers, which shall be determined as the whole number of persons in each State.

The actual Enumeration shall be made **every Term of ten Years, in the Year whose number is wholly divisible by ten, in such Manner as the Congress of the United States shall by Law direct. The Enumeration shall count each person's State of residence as of the first day of April of the Enumeration Year. The results of the Enumeration shall be reported to the President and the Speaker of the House of Representatives by the 31st day of December of the Enumeration Year. The Clerk of the House shall determine reapportionment and inform each State Governor of the number of its House Representatives by the 25th day of January of the Year following the Enumeration Year. Reapportionment shall be determined by the Method of Equal Proportions:**

1. **Let E[i] be the Enumeration for State i and let T be the Total number of seats to be apportioned (200).**
2. **Let N[i] be the Number of seats allocated to State i so far, initially setting N[i] to 1 as the mandated minimum.**
3. **Set R as the number of remaining seats to be apportioned: T minus the sum across N[i].**
4. **Set A[i] as the priority value for State i: E[i] divided by the square root of the product of N[i] and N[i]+1.**
5. **Increment N[i] by 1 seat for the State whose value A[i] is largest. Decrement R by 1.**
6. **Repeat steps 4 and 5 until R is zero. N[i] is the apportionment for State i.**

When vacancies happen in the Representation from any State, the Executive Authority thereof shall issue Writs of Election to fill such Vacancies.

The House of Representatives shall **chuse** their Speaker and other Officers; and shall have the sole Power of Impeachment.

Section 3.

The Senate of the United States shall be composed of two Senators from each State, elected by the people thereof, for six years; and each Senator shall have one Vote. **The electors in each State shall have the qualifications requisite for electors of the most numerous branch of the State legislatures.**

Immediately after they shall be assembled in Consequence of the first Election, they shall be divided as equally as may be into three Classes. The Seats of the Senators of the first Class shall be vacated at the Expiration of the second Year, of the second Class at the Expiration of the fourth Year, and of the third Class at the Expiration of the sixth Year, so that one third may be chosen every second Year.

When vacancies happen in the representation of any State in the Senate, the executive authority of such State shall issue writs of election to fill such vacancies: Provided, That the legislature of any State may empower the executive thereof to make temporary appointments until the people fill the vacancies by election as the legislature may direct.

No Person shall be a Senator who shall not have attained to the Age of thirty Years, and been nine Years a Citizen of the United States, and who shall not, when elected, be an Inhabitant of that State for which he shall be chosen.

The Vice President of the United States shall be President of the Senate, but shall have no Vote**, unless they be equally divided.**

When vacancies happen in the Representation from any State, the Executive Authority thereof shall issue Writs of Election to fill such Vacancies.

The House of Representatives shall **choose** their Speaker and other Officers; and shall have the sole Power of Impeachment.

Section 3. The Senate

The Senate of the United States shall be composed of two Senators from each State, elected by the people thereof, for six years; and each Senator shall have one Vote.

Senators shall be divided as equally as may be into three Classes. The Seats of the Senators of the first Class shall be vacated at the Expiration of the second Year, of the second Class at the Expiration of the fourth Year, and of the third Class at the Expiration of the sixth Year, so that one third may be chosen every second Year.

When vacancies happen in the representation of any State in the Senate, the executive authority of such State shall issue writs of election to fill such vacancies: Provided, That the legislature of any State may empower the executive thereof to make temporary appointments until the people fill the vacancies by election as the legislature may direct.

No Person shall be a Senator who shall not have attained to the Age of thirty Years, and been nine Years a Citizen of the United States, and who shall not, when elected, be an Inhabitant of that State for which he shall be chosen; **neither shall any Person be eligible to that Office who has been elected to that Office more than once, or has been elected to that Office once and held the office of Senator, or acted as Senator, for more than three years of a term to which some other person was elected Senator.**

The Vice President of the United States shall be President of the Senate, but shall have no Vote.

The Senate shall **chuse** their other Officers, and also a President pro tempore, in the Absence of the Vice President, or when he shall exercise the Office of President of the United States.

The Senate shall have the sole Power to try all Impeachments. When sitting for that Purpose, they shall be on Oath or Affirmation. When the President of the United States is tried, the Chief Justice shall preside: And no Person shall be convicted without the Concurrence of two thirds of the Members present.

Judgment in Cases of Impeachment shall not extend further than to removal from Office, and disqualification to hold and enjoy any Office of honor, Trust or Profit under the United States: but the Party convicted shall nevertheless be liable and subject to Indictment, Trial, Judgment and Punishment, according to Law.

Section 4.

The Times, Places and Manner of holding Elections for Senators and Representatives, shall be prescribed in each State by the Legislature thereof; but the Congress may at any time by Law make or alter such Regulations.

The terms of Senators and Representatives shall end at noon on the 3d day of January, and the terms of their successors shall then begin.

The Congress shall assemble at least once in every year, and such meeting shall begin at noon on the 3d day of January, unless they shall by law appoint a different day.

The Senate shall **choose** their other Officers, and also a President pro tempore, in the Absence of the Vice President, or when he shall exercise the Office of President of the United States.

The Senate shall have the sole Power to try all Impeachments. When sitting for that Purpose, they shall be on Oath or Affirmation. When the President of the United States is tried, the Chief Justice shall preside: And no Person shall be convicted without the Concurrence of two thirds of the Members present.

Judgment in Cases of Impeachment shall not extend further than to removal from Office, and disqualification to hold and enjoy any Office of honor, Trust or Profit under the United States: but the Party convicted shall nevertheless be liable and subject to Indictment, Trial, Judgment and Punishment, according to Law.

The Senate shall have the Power to repeal Executive Orders with the Concurrence of two thirds of the Members present.

Section 4. Congressional Elections and Terms

The Times, Places and Manner of holding Elections for Senators and Representatives, shall be prescribed in each State by the Legislature thereof; but the Congress may at any time by Law make or alter such Regulations. **Voting shall be At Large for Senators and Representatives, with ballots for voters of each State comprising all candidates of that State eligible in that Election. No information about the candidate other than name shall appear on the ballot, and each name shall not be listed more than once. The Three Star Voting method shall be used, in which the voter shall rate each candidate on a three-to-zero scale (3=Excellent, 2=Good, 1=Fair, 0=Poor). The total number shall be tallied by candidate. Candidates with the highest tallies for the available offices shall be elected. Ties shall be resolved by coin-toss of the State Governor.**

The terms of Senators and Representatives shall end at noon on the 3d day of January, and the terms of their successors shall then begin.

The Congress shall assemble at least once in every year, and such meeting shall begin at noon on the 3d day of January, unless they shall by law appoint a different day.

Section 5.

Each House shall be the Judge of the Elections, Returns and Qualifications of its own Members, and a Majority of each shall constitute a Quorum to do Business; but a smaller Number may adjourn from day to day, and may be authorized to compel the Attendance of absent Members, in such Manner, and under such Penalties as each House may provide.

Each House may determine the Rules of its Proceedings, punish its Members for disorderly **Behaviour**, and, with the Concurrence of two thirds, expel a Member.

Each House shall keep a Journal of its Proceedings, and from time to time publish the same, excepting such Parts as may in their Judgment require Secrecy; and the Yeas and Nays of the Members of either House on any question shall, at the Desire of one fifth of those Present, be entered on the Journal.

Neither House, during the Session of Congress, shall, without the Consent of the other, adjourn for more than three days, nor to any other Place than that in which the two Houses shall be sitting.

Section 6.

The Senators and Representatives shall receive a Compensation for their Services, to be ascertained by Law, and paid out of the Treasury of the United States. No law, varying the compensation for the services of the Senators and Representatives, shall take effect, until an election of Representatives shall have intervened.

The Senators and Representatives shall in all Cases, except Treason, Felony and Breach of the Peace, be privileged from Arrest during their Attendance at the Session of their respective Houses, and in going to and returning from the same; and for any Speech or Debate in either House, they shall not be questioned in any other Place.

No Senator or Representative shall, during the Time for which he was elected, be appointed to any civil Office under the Authority of the United States, which shall have been created, or

Section 5. Congressional Rules and Proceedings

Each House shall be the Judge of the Elections, Returns and Qualifications of its own Members, and a Majority of each shall constitute a Quorum to do Business; but a smaller Number may adjourn from day to day, and may be authorized to compel the Attendance of absent Members, in such Manner, and under such Penalties as each House may provide.

Each House may determine the Rules of its Proceedings, punish its Members for disorderly **Behavior**, and, with the Concurrence of two thirds, expel a Member.

Each House shall keep a Journal of its Proceedings, and from time to time publish the same, excepting such Parts as may in their Judgment require Secrecy; and the Yeas and Nays of the Members of either House on any question shall, at the Desire of one fifth of those Present, be entered on the Journal.

Neither House, during the Session of Congress, shall, without the Consent of the other, adjourn for more than three days, nor to any other Place than that in which the two Houses shall be sitting.

Section 6. Congressional Compensation, Immunity, Conflict

The Senators and Representatives shall receive a Compensation for their Services, to be ascertained by Law, and paid out of the Treasury of the United States. No law, varying the compensation for the services of the Senators and Representatives, shall take effect, until an election of Representatives shall have intervened.

The Senators and Representatives shall in all Cases, except Treason, Felony and Breach of the Peace, be privileged from Arrest during their Attendance at the Session of their respective Houses, and in going to and returning from the same; and for any Speech or Debate in either House, they shall not be questioned in any other Place.

No Senator or Representative shall, during the Time for which he was elected, be appointed to any civil Office under the Authority of the United States, which shall have been created, or the Emoluments whereof shall have been **encreased** during such time; and no Person holding any Office under the United States, shall be a Member of either House during his Continuance in Office.

Section 7.

All Bills for raising Revenue shall originate in the House of Representatives; but the Senate may propose or concur with Amendments as on other Bills.

Every Bill which shall have passed the House of Representatives and the Senate, shall, before it become a Law, be presented to the President of the United States; If he approve he shall sign it, but if not he shall return it, with his Objections to that House in which it shall have originated, who shall enter the Objections at large on their Journal, and proceed to reconsider it. If after such Reconsideration two thirds of that House shall agree to pass the Bill, it shall be sent, together with the Objections, to the other House, by which it shall likewise be reconsidered, and if approved by two thirds of that House, it shall become a Law. But in all such Cases the Votes of both Houses shall be determined by yeas and Nays, and the Names of the Persons voting for and against the Bill shall be entered on the Journal of each House respectively. If any Bill shall not be returned by the President within ten Days (Sundays excepted) after it shall have been presented to him, the Same shall be a Law, in like Manner as if he had signed it, unless the Congress by their Adjournment prevent its Return, in which Case it shall not be a Law.

Every Order, Resolution, or Vote to which the Concurrence of the Senate and House of Representatives may be necessary (except on a question of Adjournment) shall be presented to the President of the United States; and before the Same shall take Effect, shall be approved by him, or being disapproved by him, shall be repassed by two thirds of the Senate and House of the Emoluments whereof shall have been **increased** during such time; and no Person holding any Office under the United States, shall be a Member of either House during his Continuance in Office.

Section 7. Bills Becoming Laws

All Bills for raising Revenue shall originate in the House of Representatives; but the Senate may propose or concur with Amendments as on other Bills.

Every Bill which shall have passed **by two thirds of both** the House of Representatives and the Senate, shall, before it become a Law, be presented to the President of the United States; If he approve he shall sign it, but if not he shall return it, with his Objections to that House in which it shall have originated, who shall enter the Objections at large on their Journal, and proceed to reconsider it. If after such Reconsideration two thirds of that House shall agree to pass the Bill, it shall be sent, together with the Objections, to the other House, by which it shall likewise be reconsidered, and if approved by two thirds of that House, it shall become a Law. But in all such Cases the Votes of both Houses shall be determined by yeas and Nays, and the Names of the Persons voting for and against the Bill shall be entered on the Journal of each House respectively. If any Bill shall not be returned by the President within ten Days (Sundays excepted) after it shall have been presented to him, the Same shall be a Law, in like Manner as if he had signed it, unless the Congress by their Adjournment prevent its Return, in which Case it shall not be a Law.

No State or Agency or Officer of the State or Federal Government is immune from liability for violating any Act of Congress, or any provision of this Constitution unless expressly stated therein.

Every Order, Resolution, or Vote to which the Concurrence of the Senate and House of Representatives may be necessary (except on a question of Adjournment) shall be presented to the President of the United States; and before the Same shall take Effect, shall be approved by him, or being disapproved by him, shall be repassed by two thirds of the Senate and House of

Representatives, according to the Rules and Limitations prescribed in the Case of a Bill.

Section 8.

The Congress shall have Power To lay and collect Taxes, Duties, Imposts and Excises, to pay the Debts and provide for the common **Defence** and general Welfare of the United States; but all Duties, Imposts and Excises shall be uniform throughout the United States;

To borrow Money on the credit of the United States;

To regulate Commerce with foreign Nations, and among the several States, and with the Indian Tribes;

To establish **an** uniform Rule of Naturalization, and uniform Laws on the subject of Bankruptcies throughout the United States;

To coin Money, regulate the Value thereof, and of foreign Coin, and fix the Standard of Weights and Measures;

To provide for the Punishment of counterfeiting the Securities and current Coin of the United States;

To establish Post Offices and post Roads;

To promote the Progress of Science and useful Arts, by securing for limited Times to Authors and Inventors the exclusive Right to their respective Writings and Discoveries;

To constitute Tribunals inferior to the supreme Court;

To define and punish Piracies and Felonies committed on the high Seas, and Offences against the Law of Nations;

To declare War, grant Letters of Marque and Reprisal, and make Rules concerning Captures on Land and Water;

To raise and support Armies, but no Appropriation of Money to that Use shall be for a longer Term than two Years;

To provide and maintain **a Navy**;

To make Rules for the Government and Regulation of the **land and naval** Forces;

To provide for calling forth the Militia to execute the Laws of the Union, suppress Insurrections and repel Invasions;

To provide for organizing, arming, and disciplining, the Militia, and for governing such Part of them as may be employed in the Service of the United States, reserving to the States

Representatives, according to the Rules and Limitations prescribed in the Case of a Bill.

Section 8. Congressional Powers and Responsibilities

The Congress shall have Power To lay and collect Taxes, Duties, Imposts and Excises, to pay the Debts and provide for the common **Defense** and general Welfare of the United States; but all Duties, Imposts and Excises shall be uniform throughout the United States;

To borrow Money on the credit of the United States;

To regulate Commerce with foreign Nations, and among the several States, and with the Indian Tribes;

To establish **a** uniform Rule of Naturalization, and uniform Laws on the subject of Bankruptcies throughout the United States;

To coin Money, regulate the Value thereof, and of foreign Coin, and fix the Standard of Weights and Measures;

To provide for the Punishment of counterfeiting the Securities and current Coin of the United States;

To establish Post Offices and post Roads;

To promote the Progress of Science and useful Arts, by securing for limited Times to Authors and Inventors the exclusive Right to their respective Writings and Discoveries;

To constitute Tribunals inferior to the supreme Court;

To define and punish Piracies and Felonies committed on the high Seas, and Offences against the Law of Nations;

To declare War, grant Letters of Marque and Reprisal, and make Rules concerning Captures on Land and Water;

To raise and support Armies, but no Appropriation of Money to that Use shall be for a longer Term than two Years;

To provide and maintain **the Armed Forces**;

To make Rules for the Government and Regulation of the **Armed** Forces;

To provide for calling forth the Militia to execute the Laws of the Union, suppress Insurrections and repel Invasions;

To provide for organizing, arming, and disciplining, the Militia, and for governing such Part of them as may be employed in the Service of the United States, reserving to the States respectively, the Appointment of the Officers, and the Authority of training the Militia according to the discipline prescribed by Congress;

To exercise exclusive Legislation in all Cases whatsoever, over **such District (not exceeding ten Miles square) as may, by Cession of particular States, and the Acceptance of Congress, become** the Seat of the Government of the United States, and to exercise like Authority over all Places purchased by the Consent of the Legislature of the State in which the Same shall be, for the Erection of Forts, Magazines, Arsenals, dock-Yards, and other needful Buildings; -- And

To make all Laws which shall be necessary and proper for carrying into Execution the foregoing Powers, and all other Powers vested by this Constitution in the Government of the United States, or in any Department or Officer thereof.

Section 9.

The Privilege of the Writ of Habeas Corpus shall not be suspended, unless when in Cases of Rebellion or Invasion the public Safety may require it.

No Bill of Attainder or ex post facto Law shall be passed.

The Congress shall have power to lay and collect taxes on incomes, from whatever source derived, without apportionment among the several States, and without regard to any census or enumeration.

No Tax or Duty shall be laid on Articles exported from any State.

No Preference shall be given by any Regulation of Commerce or Revenue to the Ports of one State over those of another: nor shall Vessels bound to, or from, one State, be obliged to enter, clear, or pay Duties in another.

No Money shall be drawn from the Treasury, but in Consequence of Appropriations made by Law; and a regular Statement and Account of the Receipts and Expenditures of all public Money shall be published from time to time.

respectively, the Appointment of the Officers, and the Authority of training the Militia according to the discipline prescribed by Congress;

To exercise exclusive Legislation in all Cases whatsoever, over **the District that serves as** the Seat of the Government of the United States, and to exercise like Authority over all Places purchased by the Consent of the Legislature of the State in which the Same shall be, for the Erection of Forts, Magazines, Arsenals, dock-Yards, and other needful Buildings; -- And

To make all Laws which shall be necessary and proper for carrying into Execution the foregoing Powers, and all other Powers vested by this Constitution in the Government of the United States, or in any Department or Officer thereof.

Section 9. Congressional Restrictions

The Privilege of the Writ of Habeas Corpus shall not be suspended, unless when in Cases of Rebellion or Invasion the public Safety may require it.

No Bill of Attainder or ex post facto Law shall be passed.

The Congress shall have power to lay and collect taxes on incomes, from whatever source derived, without apportionment among the several States, and without regard to any census or enumeration.

No Tax or Duty shall be laid on Articles exported from any State.

No Preference shall be given by any Regulation of Commerce or Revenue to the Ports of one State over those of another: nor shall Vessels bound to, or from, one State, be obliged to enter, clear, or pay Duties in another.

No Money shall be drawn from the Treasury, but in Consequence of Appropriations made by Law; and a regular Statement and Account of the Receipts and Expenditures of all public Money shall be published from time to time.

No Money shall be drawn from the Treasury to bring the Debt of the United States, nor deposited to the Treasury to bring the Surplus of the United States, to more than four

No Title of Nobility shall be granted by the United States: And no Person holding any Office of Profit or Trust under them, shall, without the Consent of the Congress, accept of any present, Emolument, Office, or Title, of any kind whatever, from any King, Prince, or foreign State.

Section 10.

No State shall enter into any Treaty, Alliance, or Confederation; grant Letters of Marque and Reprisal; coin Money; emit Bills of Credit; make any Thing **but gold and silver Coin** a Tender in Payment of Debts; pass any Bill of Attainder, ex post facto Law, or Law impairing the Obligation of Contracts, or grant any Title of Nobility.

No State shall, without the Consent of the Congress, lay any Imposts or Duties on Imports or Exports, except what may be absolutely necessary for executing it's inspection Laws: and the net Produce of all Duties and Imposts, laid by any State on Imports or Exports, shall be for the Use of the Treasury of the United States; and all such Laws shall be subject to the Revision and **Controul** of the Congress.

No State shall, without the Consent of Congress, lay any Duty of Tonnage, keep Troops, or Ships of War in time of Peace, enter into any Agreement or Compact with another State, or with a foreign Power, or engage in War, unless actually invaded, or in such imminent Danger as will not admit of delay.

Goldars times the population as of the most recent ten-year Enumeration. The exception is that from the twenty-year period from 20xx to 20yy, the Debt may be as high as the Enumeration population times the greater of four or the product of (20yy-yyyy) times 40.345 divided by 20, where yyyy is the year of withdrawal.

No Title of Nobility shall be granted by the United States: And no Person holding any Office of Profit or Trust under them, shall, without the Consent of the Congress, accept of any present, Emolument, Office, or Title, of any kind whatever, from any King, Prince, or foreign State.

Section 10. State Restrictions

No State shall enter into any Treaty, Alliance, or Confederation; grant Letters of Marque and Reprisal; coin Money; emit Bills of Credit; make any Thing a Tender in Payment of Debts; pass any Bill of Attainder, ex post facto Law, or Law impairing the Obligation of Contracts, or grant any Title of Nobility.

No State shall, without the Consent of the Congress, lay any Imposts or Duties on Imports or Exports, except what may be absolutely necessary for executing it's inspection Laws: and the net Produce of all Duties and Imposts, laid by any State on Imports or Exports, shall be for the Use of the Treasury of the United States; and all such Laws shall be subject to the Revision and **Control** of the Congress.

No State shall, without the Consent of Congress, lay any Duty of Tonnage, keep Troops, or Ships of War in time of Peace, enter into any Agreement or Compact with another State, or with a foreign Power, or engage in War, unless actually invaded, or in such imminent Danger as will not admit of delay.

Article II.

Section 1.

The executive Power shall be vested in a President of the United States of America. He shall hold his Office during the Term of four Years, and, together with the Vice President, chosen for the same Term, be elected, **as follows:**

Each State shall appoint, in such Manner as the Legislature thereof may direct, a Number of Electors, equal to the whole Number of Senators and Representatives to which the State may be entitled in the Congress: but no Senator or Representative, or Person holding an Office of Trust or Profit under the United States, shall be appointed an Elector.

The District constituting the seat of Government of the United States shall appoint in such manner as the Congress may direct:

A number of electors of President and Vice President equal to the whole number of Senators and Representatives in Congress to which the District would be entitled if it were a State, but in no event more than the least populous State; they shall be in addition to those appointed by the States, but they shall be considered, for the purposes of the election of President and Vice President, to be electors appointed by a State; and they shall meet in the District and perform such duties as provided in this Section.

The Electors shall meet in their respective states and vote by ballot for President and Vice-President, one of whom, at least, shall not be an inhabitant of the same state with themselves; they shall name in their ballots the person voted for as President, and in distinct ballots the person voted for as Vice-President, and they shall make distinct lists of all persons voted for as President, and of all persons voted for as Vice-President, and of the number of votes for each, which lists they shall sign and certify, and transmit sealed to the seat of the government of the United States, directed to the President of the Senate; -- the President of the Senate shall, in the presence of the Senate and House of Representatives, open all the certificates and the votes shall then be counted; -- The person having the greatest number of votes for

Article II. President – The Executive Branch

Section 1. The President and Vice President

The executive Power shall be vested in a President of the United States of America. He shall hold his Office during the Term of four Years, and, together with the Vice President, chosen for the same Term, be elected **by the citizens of the United States and of the District constituting the seat of Government of the United States.**

President, shall be the President, if such number be a majority of the whole number of Electors appointed; and if no person have such majority, then from the persons having the highest numbers not exceeding three on the list of those voted for as President, the House of Representatives shall choose immediately, by ballot, the President. But in choosing the President, the votes shall be taken by states, the representation from each state having one vote; a quorum for this purpose shall consist of a member or members from two-thirds of the states, and a majority of all the states shall be necessary to a choice.

The person having the greatest number of votes as Vice-President, shall be the Vice-President, if such number be a majority of the whole number of Electors appointed, and if no person have a majority, then from the two highest numbers on the list, the Senate shall choose the Vice-President; a quorum for the purpose shall consist of two-thirds of the whole number of Senators, and a majority of the whole number shall be necessary to a choice. But no person constitutionally ineligible to the office of President shall be eligible to that of Vice-President of the United States.

If, at the time fixed for the beginning of the term of the President, the President elect shall have died, the Vice President elect shall become President. If a President shall not have been chosen before the time fixed for the beginning of his term, or if the President elect shall have failed to qualify, then the Vice President elect shall act as President until a President shall have qualified; and the Congress may by law provide for the case wherein neither a President elect nor a Vice President elect shall have qualified, declaring who shall then act as President, or the manner in which one who is to act shall be selected, and such person shall act accordingly until a President or Vice President shall have qualified.

The Congress may by law provide for the case of the death of any of the persons from whom the House of Representatives may choose a President whenever the right of choice shall have devolved upon them, and for the case of the death of any of the persons from whom the Senate may choose a Vice President whenever the right of choice shall have devolved upon them.

If, at the time fixed for the beginning of the term of the President, the President elect shall have died, the Vice President elect shall become President. If a President shall not have been chosen before the time fixed for the beginning of his term, or if the President elect shall have failed to qualify, then the Vice President elect shall act as President until a President shall have qualified; and the Congress may by law provide for the case wherein neither a President elect nor a Vice President elect shall have qualified, declaring who shall then act as President, or the manner in which one who is to act shall be selected, and such person shall act accordingly until a President or Vice President shall have qualified.

The Congress may by law provide for the case of the death of any of the persons from whom the House of Representatives may choose a President whenever the right of choice shall have devolved upon them, and for the case of the death of any of the persons from whom the Senate may choose a Vice President whenever the right of choice shall have devolved upon them.

The Congress may determine the Time of chusing the Electors, and the Day on which they shall give their Votes; which Day shall be the same throughout the United States.

The terms of the President and the Vice President shall end at noon on the 20th day of January, and the terms of their successors shall then begin.

No Person except a natural born Citizen, or a Citizen of the United States, **at the time of the Adoption of this Constitution,** shall be eligible to the Office of President; neither shall any Person be eligible to that Office who shall not have attained to the Age of thirty-five Years, and been fourteen Years a Resident within the United States; neither shall any Person be eligible to that Office who has been elected to that Office more than once, or has been elected to that Office once and held the office of President, or acted as President, for more than two years of a term to which some other person was elected President. **But this Article shall not apply to any person holding the office of President when this Article was proposed by the Congress, and shall not prevent any person who may be holding the office of President, or acting as President, during the term within which this Article becomes operative from holding the office of President or acting as President during the remainder of such term.**

In case of the removal of the President from office or of his death or resignation, the Vice President shall become President.

Whenever there is a vacancy in the office of the Vice President, the President shall nominate a Vice President who shall take office upon confirmation by a majority vote of both Houses of Congress.

Whenever the President transmits to the President pro tempore of the Senate and the Speaker of the House of Representatives his written declaration that he is unable to discharge the powers and duties of his office, and until he transmits to them a written declaration to the contrary, such powers and duties shall be discharged by the Vice President as Acting President.

Whenever the Vice President and a majority of either the principal officers of the executive departments or of such other body as Congress may by law provide, transmit to the President pro tempore of the Senate and the Speaker of the House of Representatives their written declaration that the President is unable

The terms of the President and the Vice President shall end at noon on the 20th day of January, and the terms of their successors shall then begin.

No Person except a natural born Citizen, or a Citizen of the United States, shall be eligible to the Office of President; neither shall any Person be eligible to that Office who shall not have attained to the Age of thirty-five Years, and been fourteen Years a Resident within the United States; neither shall any Person be eligible to that Office who has been elected to that Office more than once, or has been elected to that Office once and held the office of President, or acted as President, for more than two years of a term to which some other person was elected President.

In case of the removal of the President from office or of his death or resignation, the Vice President shall become President.

Whenever there is a vacancy in the office of the Vice President, the President shall nominate a Vice President who shall take office upon confirmation by a majority vote of both Houses of Congress.

Whenever the President transmits to the President pro tempore of the Senate and the Speaker of the House of Representatives his written declaration that he is unable to discharge the powers and duties of his office, and until he transmits to them a written declaration to the contrary, such powers and duties shall be discharged by the Vice President as Acting President.

Whenever the Vice President and a majority of either the principal officers of the executive departments or of such other body as Congress may by law provide, transmit to the President pro tempore of the Senate and the Speaker of the House of Representatives their written declaration that the President is unable to discharge the powers and duties of his office, the Vice President shall immediately assume the powers and duties of the office as Acting President.

Thereafter, when the President transmits to the President pro tempore of the Senate and the Speaker of the House of Representatives his written declaration that no inability exists, he shall resume the powers and duties of his office unless the Vice President and a majority of either the principal officers of the executive department or of such other body as Congress may by law provide, transmit within four days to the President pro tempore of the Senate and the Speaker of the House of Representatives their written declaration that the President is unable to discharge the powers and duties of his office. Thereupon Congress shall decide the issue, assembling within forty-eight hours for that purpose if not in session. If the Congress, within twenty-one days after receipt of the latter written declaration, or, if Congress is not in session, within twenty-one days after Congress is required to assemble, determines by two-thirds vote of both Houses that the President is unable to discharge the powers and duties of his office, the Vice President shall continue to discharge the same as Acting President; otherwise, the President shall resume the powers and duties of his office.

The President shall, at stated Times, receive for his Services, a Compensation, which shall neither be **encreased** nor diminished during the Period for which he shall have been elected, and he shall not receive within that Period any other Emolument from the United States, or any of them.

Before he enter on the Execution of his Office, he shall take the following Oath or Affirmation: -- "I do solemnly swear (or affirm) that I will faithfully execute the Office of President of the United States, and will to the best of my Ability, preserve, protect and defend the Constitution of the United States."

Section 2.

The President shall be Commander in Chief of the **Army and Navy** of the United States, and of the Militia of the several States, when called into the actual Service of the United States; he may require the Opinion, in writing, of the principal Officer to discharge the powers and duties of his office, the Vice President shall immediately assume the powers and duties of the office as Acting President.

Thereafter, when the President transmits to the President pro tempore of the Senate and the Speaker of the House of Representatives his written declaration that no inability exists, he shall resume the powers and duties of his office unless the Vice President and a majority of either the principal officers of the executive department or of such other body as Congress may by law provide, transmit within four days to the President pro tempore of the Senate and the Speaker of the House of Representatives their written declaration that the President is unable to discharge the powers and duties of his office. Thereupon Congress shall decide the issue, assembling within forty-eight hours for that purpose if not in session. If the Congress, within twenty-one days after receipt of the latter written declaration, or, if Congress is not in session, within twenty-one days after Congress is required to assemble, determines by two-thirds vote of both Houses that the President is unable to discharge the powers and duties of his office, the Vice President shall continue to discharge the same as Acting President; otherwise, the President shall resume the powers and duties of his office.

The President shall, at stated Times, receive for his Services, a Compensation, which shall neither be **increased** nor diminished during the Period for which he shall have been elected, and he shall not receive within that Period any other Emolument from the United States, or any of them.

Before he enter on the Execution of his Office, he shall take the following Oath or Affirmation: -- "I do solemnly swear (or affirm) that I will faithfully execute the Office of President of the United States, and will to the best of my Ability, preserve, protect and defend the Constitution of the United States."

Section 2. Commander in Chief

The President shall be Commander in Chief of the **Armed Forces** of the United States, and of the Militia of the several States, when called into the actual Service of the United States; he may require the Opinion, in writing, of the principal Officer in each of the executive Departments, upon any Subject relating to the Duties of their respective Offices, **and he shall have Power to grant Reprieves and Pardons for Offences against the United States, except in Cases of Impeachment.**

He shall have Power, by and with the Advice and Consent of the Senate, to make Treaties, provided two thirds of the Senators present concur; and he shall nominate, and by and with the Advice and Consent of the Senate, shall appoint Ambassadors, other public Ministers and Consuls, **Judges of the supreme Court,** and all other Officers of the United States, whose Appointments are not herein otherwise provided for, and which shall be established by Law: but the Congress may by Law vest the Appointment of such inferior Officers, as they think proper, in the President alone, in the Courts of Law, or in the Heads of Departments.

The President shall have Power to fill up all Vacancies that may happen during the Recess of the Senate, by granting Commissions which shall expire at the End of their next Session.

Section 3.

He shall from time to time give to the Congress Information of the State of the Union, and recommend to their Consideration such Measures as he shall judge necessary and expedient; he may, on extraordinary Occasions, convene both Houses, or either of them, and in Case of Disagreement between them, with Respect to the Time of Adjournment, he may adjourn them to such Time as he shall think proper; he shall receive Ambassadors and other public Ministers; **he shall take Care that the Laws be faithfully executed, and shall Commission all the Officers of the United States.**

in each of the executive Departments, upon any Subject relating to the Duties of their respective Offices.

He shall have Power, by and with the Advice and Consent of the Senate, to make Treaties, provided two thirds of the Senators present concur; and he shall nominate, and by and with the Advice and Consent of the Senate, shall appoint Ambassadors, other public Ministers and Consuls, and all other Officers of the United States, whose Appointments are not herein otherwise provided for, and which shall be established by Law: but the Congress may by Law vest the Appointment of such inferior Officers, as they think proper, in the President alone, in the Courts of Law, or in the Heads of Departments.

The President shall have Power to fill up all Vacancies that may happen during the Recess of the Senate, by granting Commissions which shall expire at the End of their next Session.
On the 1st day of March of each Year wholly divisible by two, the President shall nominate, and by and with the Advice and Consent of the Senate, shall appoint one Judge to the supreme Court, provided two thirds of the Senators present concur. No Judge having previously served on the supreme Court shall be reappointed. The Judge so appointed shall fill an open vacancy if one exists, else shall replace the Justice having served longest on the supreme Court.

Section 3. Duties of the President

He shall from time to time give to the Congress Information of the State of the Union, and recommend to their Consideration such Measures as he shall judge necessary and expedient; he may, on extraordinary Occasions, convene both Houses, or either of them, and in Case of Disagreement between them, with Respect to the Time of Adjournment, he may adjourn them to such Time as he shall think proper; he shall receive Ambassadors and other public Ministers; **he shall Commission all the Officers of the United States; he shall take Care that the Laws be faithfully executed and shall issue Executive Orders in**

Section 4.

The President, Vice President and all civil Officers of the United States, shall be removed from Office on Impeachment for, and Conviction of, Treason, Bribery, or other high Crimes and Misdemeanors.

Article III.

Section 1.

The judicial Power of the United States, shall be vested in one supreme Court, and in such inferior Courts as the Congress may from time to time ordain and establish. The Judges, both of the supreme and inferior Courts, shall hold their Offices during good **Behaviour**, and shall, at stated Times, receive for their Services, a Compensation, which shall not be diminished during their Continuance in Office.

furtherance of such duty that have the force of Law provided two thirds of the Senators present concur; he shall have Power to repeal Executive Orders.

Section 4. Impeachment

The President, Vice President and all civil Officers of the United States, shall be removed from Office on Impeachment for, and Conviction of, Treason, Bribery, or other high Crimes and Misdemeanors.

Section 5. Goldar

A Goldar is a number of U.S. dollars at a point in time. The exact number shall be set by the Secretary of Treasury of the United States on the 1st day of January of each year, based on the prevailing price of one ounce of gold. The number is effective for that calendar year. Any reference to a Goldar assumes its value as of the date of the applicable financial transaction.

Article III. Supreme Court – The Judicial Branch

Section 1. Composition of Supreme Court

The judicial Power of the United States, shall be vested in one supreme Court **having nine members one of whom shall be designated as Chief Justice by its members**, and in such inferior Courts as the Congress may from time to time ordain and establish. The Judges, both of the supreme and inferior Courts, shall hold their Offices during good **Behavior**, and shall, at stated Times, receive for their Services, a Compensation, which shall not be diminished during their Continuance in Office. **When vacancies happen in the supreme Court, they shall remain unfilled until the biannual Presidential appointment and Senate confirmation.**

Section 2.

The judicial Power shall extend to all Cases, in Law and Equity, arising under this Constitution, the Laws of the United States, and Treaties made, or which shall be made, under their Authority; -- to all Cases affecting Ambassadors, other public Ministers and Consuls; -- to all Cases of admiralty and maritime Jurisdiction; -- to Controversies to which the United States shall be a Party; -- to Controversies between two or more States; -- between Citizens of different States; -- between Citizens of the same State claiming Lands under Grants of different States. **The Judicial Power of the United States shall not be construed to extend to any suit in law or equity, commenced or prosecuted against one of the United States by Citizens of another State, or by Citizens or Subjects of any Foreign State.**

In all Cases affecting Ambassadors, other public Ministers and Consuls, and those in which a State shall be Party, the supreme Court shall have original Jurisdiction. In all the other Cases before mentioned, the supreme Court shall have appellate Jurisdiction, both as to Law and Fact, with such Exceptions, and under such Regulations as the Congress shall make.

The Trial of all Crimes, except in Cases of Impeachment, shall be by Jury; and such Trial shall be held in the State where the said Crimes shall have been committed; but when not committed within any State, the Trial shall be at such Place or Places as the Congress may by Law have directed.

Section 2. Duties of Supreme Court

The judicial Power shall extend to all Cases, in Law and Equity, arising under this Constitution, the Laws of the United States, and Treaties made, or which shall be made, under their Authority; -- to all Cases affecting Ambassadors, other public Ministers and Consuls; -- to all Cases of admiralty and maritime Jurisdiction; -- to Controversies to which the United States shall be a Party; -- to Controversies between two or more States; -- **between a State and Citizens of another State,** -- between Citizens of different States, -- between Citizens of the same State claiming Lands under Grants of different States, **and between a State, or the Citizens thereof, and foreign States, Citizens or Subjects.**

In all Cases affecting Ambassadors, other public Ministers and Consuls, and those in which a State shall be Party, the supreme Court shall have original Jurisdiction. In all the other Cases before mentioned, the supreme Court shall have appellate Jurisdiction, both as to Law and Fact, with such Exceptions, and under such Regulations as the Congress shall make.

The Trial of all Crimes, except in Cases of Impeachment, shall be by Jury; and such Trial shall be held in the State where the said Crimes shall have been committed; but when not committed within any State, the Trial shall be at such Place or Places as the Congress may by Law have directed.

The supreme Court, with Concurrence of two thirds of its members, shall have Power to grant Reprieves and Pardons for Offences against the United States, except in Cases of Impeachment.

Section 3.

Treason against the United States, shall consist only in levying War against them, or in adhering to their Enemies, giving them Aid and Comfort. No Person shall be convicted of Treason unless on the Testimony of two Witnesses to the same overt Act, or on Confession in open Court.

The Congress shall have Power to declare the Punishment of Treason, but no Attainder of Treason shall work Corruption of Blood, or Forfeiture except during the Life of the Person attainted.

Article IV.

Section 1.

Full Faith and Credit shall be given in each State to the public Acts, Records, and judicial Proceedings of every other State. And the Congress may by general Laws prescribe the Manner in which such Acts, Records and Proceedings shall be proved, and the Effect thereof.

Section 2.

All persons born or naturalized in the United States, and subject to the jurisdiction thereof, are citizens of the United States and of the State wherein they reside. No State shall make or enforce any law which shall abridge the privileges or immunities of citizens of the United States; nor shall any State deprive any person of life, liberty, or property, without due process of law; nor deny to any person within its jurisdiction the equal protection of the laws. **The right of citizens of the United States to vote shall not be denied or abridged by the United States or by**

Section 3. Treason

Treason against the United States, shall consist only in levying War against them, or in adhering to their Enemies, giving them Aid and Comfort. No Person shall be convicted of Treason unless on the Testimony of two Witnesses to the same overt Act, or on Confession in open Court.

The Congress shall have Power to declare the Punishment of Treason, but no Attainder of Treason shall work Corruption of Blood, or Forfeiture except during the Life of the Person attainted.

Article IV. Rules and Procedures

Section 1. State Reciprocation

Full Faith and Credit shall be given in each State to the public Acts, Records, and judicial Proceedings of every other State. And the Congress may by general Laws prescribe the Manner in which such Acts, Records and Proceedings shall be proved, and the Effect thereof.

A Person charged in any State with Treason, Felony, or other Crime, who shall flee from Justice, and be found in another State, shall on Demand of the executive Authority of the State from which he fled, be delivered up, to be removed to the State having Jurisdiction of the Crime.

Section 2. Citizenship

All persons born or naturalized in the United States, and subject to the jurisdiction thereof, are citizens of the United States and of the State wherein they reside. No State shall make or enforce any law which shall abridge the privileges or immunities of citizens of the United States; nor shall any State deprive any person of life, liberty, or property, without due process of law; nor deny to any person within its jurisdiction the equal protection of the laws. **Citizens having attained the age of eighteen years shall be permitted to vote. The right of citizens of the United**

any State on account of race, color, sex, or previous condition of servitude. The right of citizens of the United States to vote in any primary or other election for President or Vice President, for electors for President or Vice President, or for Senator or Representative in Congress, shall not be denied or abridged by the United States or any State by reason of failure to pay any poll tax or other tax.

The Citizens of each State shall be entitled to all Privileges and Immunities of Citizens in the several States.

A Person charged in any State with Treason, Felony, or other Crime, who shall flee from Justice, and be found in another State, shall on Demand of the executive Authority of the State from which he fled, be delivered up, to be removed to the State having Jurisdiction of the Crime.

Neither slavery nor involuntary servitude, except as a punishment for crime whereof the party shall have been duly convicted, shall exist within the United States, or any place subject to their jurisdiction.

Section 3.

New States may be admitted by the Congress into this Union; but no new State shall be formed or erected within the Jurisdiction of any other State; nor any State be formed by the Junction of two or more States, or Parts of States, without the Consent of the Legislatures of the States concerned as well as of the Congress.

The Congress shall have Power to dispose of and make all needful Rules and Regulations respecting the Territory or other Property belonging to the United States; and nothing in this Constitution shall be so construed as to Prejudice any Claims of the United States, or of any particular State.

Section 4.

The United States shall guarantee to every State in this Union a Republican Form of Government, and shall protect each of them against Invasion; and on Application of the Legislature, or

States to vote in any primary or other election for President or Vice President or Senator or Representative in Congress, shall not be denied or abridged by the United States or by any State by reason of failure to pay any poll tax or other tax, or for any reason except age if under eighteen years.

The Citizens of each State shall be entitled to all Privileges and Immunities of Citizens in the several States.

A Person charged in any State with Treason, Felony, or other Crime, who shall flee from Justice, and be found in another State, shall on Demand of the executive Authority of the State from which he fled, be delivered up, to be removed to the State having Jurisdiction of the Crime.

Neither slavery nor involuntary servitude, except as a punishment for crime whereof the party shall have been duly convicted, shall exist within the United States, or any place subject to their jurisdiction.

Section 3. **State Admission**

New States may be admitted by the Congress into this Union; but no new State shall be formed or erected within the Jurisdiction of any other State; nor any State be formed by the Junction of two or more States, or Parts of States, without the Consent of the Legislatures of the States concerned as well as of the Congress.

The Congress shall have Power to dispose of and make all needful Rules and Regulations respecting the Territory or other Property belonging to the United States; and nothing in this Constitution shall be so construed as to Prejudice any Claims of the United States, or of any particular State.

Section 4. **Obligation to the States**

The United States shall guarantee to every State in this Union a Republican Form of Government, and shall protect each of them against Invasion; and on Application of the Legislature, or of the Executive (when the Legislature cannot be convened) against domestic Violence.

Section x. (Amendments I and IX)

Congress shall make no law respecting an establishment of religion, or prohibiting the free exercise thereof; or abridging the freedom of speech, or of the press; or the right of the people peaceably to assemble, and to petition the Government for a redress of grievances.

The enumeration in the Constitution, of certain rights, shall not be construed to deny or disparage others retained by the people.

Section x. (Amendments II and III)

A well regulated Militia, being necessary to the security of a free State, the right of the people to keep and bear Arms, shall not be infringed.

No Soldier shall, in time of peace be quartered in any house, without the consent of the Owner, nor in time of war, but in a manner to be prescribed by law.

Section x. (Amendments IV to VIII)

The right of the people to be secure in their persons, houses, papers, and effects, against unreasonable searches and seizures, shall not be violated, and no Warrants shall issue, but upon probable cause, supported by Oath or affirmation, and particularly describing the place to be searched, and the persons or things to be seized.

No person shall be held to answer for a capital, or otherwise infamous crime, unless on a presentment or indictment of a Grand Jury, except in cases arising in the **land or naval** forces, or in the Militia, when in actual service in time of War or public danger; nor shall any person be subject for the same offence to be twice put in jeopardy of life or limb; nor shall be compelled in of the Executive (when the Legislature cannot be convened) against domestic Violence.

Section 5. Freedom of Expression

Given that Tyranny suffers at the Voice of Free People and that this Constitution is the embodiment of that Voice, Congress shall make no law abridging freedom of expression that does not cause or incite destruction or injury and is not false and defamatory, such expression including religious exercise, freedom of speech or of the press, assembly of the people, and petitioning the Government for a redress of grievances.

Section 6. Justice

The right of the people to be secure in their persons, houses, papers, and effects, against unreasonable searches and seizures, shall not be violated, and no Warrants shall issue, but upon probable cause, supported by Oath or affirmation, and particularly describing the place to be searched, and the persons or things to be seized.

No person shall be held to answer for a capital, or otherwise infamous crime, unless on a presentment or indictment of a Grand Jury, except in cases arising in the **armed** forces, or in the Militia, when in actual service in time of War or public danger; nor shall any person be subject for the same offence to be twice put in jeopardy of life or limb; nor shall be compelled in any

any criminal case to be a witness against himself, nor be deprived of life, liberty, or property, without due process of law; nor shall private property be taken for public use, without just compensation.

In all criminal prosecutions, the accused shall enjoy the right to a speedy and public trial, by an impartial jury of the State and district wherein the crime shall have been committed, which district shall have been previously ascertained by law, and to be informed of the nature and cause of the accusation; to be confronted with the witnesses against him; to have compulsory process for obtaining witnesses in his favor, and to have the Assistance of Counsel for his **defence**.

In Suits at common law, where the value in controversy shall exceed **twenty dollars**, the right of trial by jury shall be preserved, and no fact tried by a jury, shall be otherwise reexamined in any Court of the United States, than according to the rules of the common law.

Excessive bail shall not be required, nor excessive fines imposed, nor cruel and unusual punishments inflicted.

Section x. (Amendment XIV, Section 3)

No person shall be a Senator or Representative in Congress, or elector of President and Vice-President, or hold any office, civil or military, under the United States, or under any State, who, having previously taken an oath, as a member of Congress, or as an officer of the United States, or as a member of any State legislature, or as an executive or judicial officer of any State, to support the Constitution of the United States, shall have engaged in insurrection or rebellion against the same, or given aid or comfort to the enemies thereof. But Congress may by a vote of two-thirds of each House, remove such disability.

criminal case to be a witness against himself, nor be deprived of life, liberty, or property, without due process of law; nor shall private property be taken for public use, without just compensation.

In all criminal prosecutions, the accused shall enjoy the right to a speedy and public trial, by an impartial jury of the State and district wherein the crime shall have been committed, which district shall have been previously ascertained by law, and to be informed of the nature and cause of the accusation; to be confronted with the witnesses against him; to have compulsory process for obtaining witnesses in his favor, and to have the Assistance of Counsel for his **defense**.

In Suits at common law, where the value in controversy shall exceed **one Goldar**, the right of trial by jury shall be preserved, and no fact tried by a jury, shall be otherwise re-examined in any Court of the United States, than according to the rules of the common law.

Excessive bail shall not be required, nor excessive fines imposed, nor cruel and unusual punishments inflicted.

No State shall make or enforce any law which shall abridge the provisions of this Section.

Section 7. Violation of Oath

No person shall be a Senator or Representative in Congress, or elector of President and Vice-President, or hold any office, civil or military, under the United States, or under any State, who, having previously taken an oath, as a member of Congress, or as an officer of the United States, or as a member of any State legislature, or as an executive or judicial officer of any State, to support the Constitution of the United States, shall have engaged in insurrection or rebellion against the same, or given aid or comfort to the enemies thereof. But Congress may by a vote of two-thirds of each House, remove such disability.

Section x. (Amendment XIV, Section 4)

The validity of the public debt of the United States, authorized by law, including debts incurred for payment of pensions and bounties for services in suppressing insurrection or rebellion, shall not be questioned. But neither the United States nor any State shall assume or pay any debt or obligation incurred in aid of insurrection or rebellion against the United States, **or any claim for the loss or emancipation of any slave;** but all such debts, obligations and claims shall be held illegal and void.

Section x. (Amendments IX and X)

The enumeration in the Constitution, of certain rights, shall not be construed to deny or disparage others retained by the people. The powers not delegated to the United States by the Constitution, nor prohibited by it to the States, are reserved to the States respectively, or to the people.

Section 8. Public Debt

The validity of the public debt of the United States, authorized by law, including debts incurred for payment of pensions and bounties for services in suppressing insurrection or rebellion, shall not be questioned. But neither the United States nor any State shall assume or pay any debt or obligation incurred in aid of insurrection or rebellion against the United States; but all such debts, obligations and claims shall be held illegal and void.

Section 9. Founding Principles

The enumeration in the Constitution, of certain rights, shall not be construed to deny or disparage others retained by the people. The powers not delegated to the United States by the Constitution, nor prohibited by it to the States, are reserved to the States respectively, or to the people.

Section 10. Elections

A Federal Election Commission (the Commission) shall be established by Congress to administer and enforce Federal campaign and election laws.

Candidates for offices of President, Senator, and Representative shall submit to the Commission by the first day of December prior to that election year an application which shall include name, contact information, office sought, and required qualifications. Campaign donations shall be used exclusively for activities relating to the candidate's campaign in that election. Within 60 days following the general election, residual campaign donations shall be returned by the candidate's committee to campaign donors pro rata.

By the first of January of the election year, the Commission shall publish the names and offices of Candidates so Registered.

On the first Tuesday following the first Monday of February of the election year, the Qualification Election shall be

held, in which Voters shall from the lists of Registered Candidates attest to as many as eight for President, six times the number of open Senate seats in the State for Senator, and three times the number of Representatives apportioned to the State for Representative. Candidates qualify for the Primary Election who receive sufficient attestations, the number so required depending on the office sought, upon the United States and separate State Populations from the most recent ten-year Enumeration, and upon the most recent Representative apportionment by State: for President, the product of 0.002 and the U.S. Population; for Representative, the product of 0.005 and the State Population divided by the number of the State's Representatives; for Senator, the product of 0.005, the State Population, and the square-root of the number of Representatives apportioned to the State, then divided by the number of that State's Representatives.

Qualified Candidates shall submit to the Commission by the first day of March of that election year a written campaign statement designated for public release, that statement being rendered in plain text and being no longer than two thousand words, and a written list of five questions to be posed to opposing Candidates.

By the first day of April of that election year, Candidates shall sit for video recording of campaign remarks, such recording administered under the direction of the Commission, having a common backdrop for all Candidates, with no music or special effects, and lasting no more than ten minutes. At the same sitting, the Candidate shall be recorded responding to ten, or fewer if unavailable, written questions from opponent Candidates, those questions selected randomly by and known only to the Commission, its only discretion being to remove perceived duplicates. The Candidate is allowed sixty seconds from receipt of each question to respond, and each response may last no more than five minutes.

By the first day of May of that election year, the Federal Election Commission shall make such written statements, video statements, and video responses freely and readily available to all U.S. citizens.

On the first Tuesday following the first Monday of June of the election year, the Primary Election shall be held, in

which Voters shall award each Qualified Candidate 3 (Great), 2 (Good), 2 (Fair), or 0 (Poor). Candidates qualify for the General Election whose total tally for President is in the top eight, for Senator is in the top six times the number of open Senate seats for the State, and for Representative is in the top three times the number of Representatives apportioned to that State.

By the first day of July of that election year, remaining Candidates shall at their option submit to the Commission revisions to their written campaign statement, and to their written list of five questions to be posed to opposing Candidates.

By the first day of August of that election year, the Candidate shall be recorded responding to ten, or fewer if unavailable, revised questions from opponent Candidates. At the same sitting, Candidates shall at their option sit for a revised video recording of campaign remarks.

By the first day of September of that election year, the Federal Election Commission shall make both original and revised written statements, video statements, and video responses freely and readily available to all U.S. citizens.

By the first day of October of that election year, Candidates for President shall select a Vice President whose name shall join theirs on the General Election ballot. Having one's name on that ballot as President shall not preclude the Candidate having his or her name once or more on the ballot as Vice President.

On the first Tuesday following the first Monday of November of the election year, the General Election for offices of President/Vice President, Senators, and Representatives shall be held, in which Voters shall award each Candidate 3 (Great), 2 (Good), 2 (Fair), or 0 (Poor). Candidates with the highest tallies shall fill the open seats. If two Senate seats are open for a State, the elected Senator with highest tally shall choose the seat to fill.

Section 11. Emoluments

Within thirty days of taking office, each President,

Section x. (Amendment XIV, Section 5)

The Congress shall have power to enforce, by appropriate legislation, the provisions of this article.

Senator, Representative, and Supreme Court Justice shall present to the Federal Election Commission an accounting of the value of his estate as of the date of approval, confirmation, or election. Within thirty days of the final day in office, he shall provide a final accounting of the value of his estate as of the date of termination, including amounts accrued, pledged, or constructively owned but held by others, and an accounting of the value of perquisites while in office beyond the Compensation for his Services as ascertained by Law. Within 90 days, the Federal Election Commission shall provide an assessment of the amount deemed attributable to the office held. The amount shall be remitted by the ex-official or his estate to the U.S. Treasury within 180 days of the assessment. The portion of the amount held by others or having appearance of quid pro quo shall be so indicated in the assessment, and its value doubled upon remission. Penalties from these assessments shall not extend further than these remissions, but the Party so penalized shall nevertheless be liable and subject to Indictment, Trial, Judgment and Punishment, according to Law.

Section 12. Excess Wealth

To preclude abuse inherent in the power of excess wealth, citizens are limited to 40,000 Goldars of constructively owned assets, as determined at each year-end. Excess shall be taxed at 80% payable to the United States Treasury by the 15th day of April following the year-end. The exception is that from the seven years from year-end 20xx to year-end 20yy, the tax rate is the lesser of 80% or ten times (yyyy-20xx) where yyyy is the current year-end.

Section 13. Enforcement

Congress shall have power to enforce this Article by appropriate legislation.

Article V.

The Congress, whenever two thirds of both Houses shall deem it necessary, shall propose Amendments to this Constitution, or, on the Application of the Legislatures of two thirds of the several States, shall call a Convention for proposing Amendments, which, in either Case, shall be valid to all Intents and Purposes, as Part of this Constitution, when ratified by the Legislatures of three fourths of the several States, or by Conventions in three fourths thereof, as the one or the other Mode of Ratification may be proposed by the Congress; Provided that no Amendment which may be made prior to the Year One thousand eight hundred and eight shall in any Manner affect the first and fourth Clauses in the Ninth Section of the first Article; and that no State, without its Consent, shall be deprived of its equal Suffrage in the Senate.

Article VI.

All Debts contracted and Engagements entered into, before the Adoption of this Constitution, shall be as valid against the United States under this Constitution, as under the Confederation.

This Constitution, and the Laws of the United States which shall be made in Pursuance thereof; and all Treaties made, or which shall be made, under the Authority of the United States, shall be the supreme Law of the Land; and the Judges in every State shall be bound thereby, any Thing in the Constitution or Laws of any State to the Contrary notwithstanding.

The Senators and Representatives before mentioned, and the Members of the several State Legislatures, and all executive and judicial Officers, both of the United States and of the several States, shall be bound by Oath or Affirmation, to support this Constitution; but no religious Test shall ever be required as a

Article V. Amendments

The Congress, whenever two thirds of both Houses shall deem it necessary, shall propose Amendments to this Constitution, or, on the Application of the Legislatures of two thirds of the several States, shall call a Convention for proposing Amendments, which, in either Case, shall be valid to all Intents and Purposes, as Part of this Constitution, when ratified by the Legislatures of three fourths of the several States, or by Conventions in three fourths thereof, as the one or the other Mode of Ratification may be proposed by the Congress; Provided that no Amendment which may be made prior to the Year One thousand eight hundred and eight shall in any Manner affect the first and fourth Clauses in the Ninth Section of the first Article; and that no State, without its Consent, shall be deprived of its equal Suffrage in the Senate.

Article VI. Supreme Law

This Constitution, and the Laws of the United States which shall be made in Pursuance thereof; and all Treaties made, or which shall be made, under the Authority of the United States, shall be the supreme Law of the Land; and the Judges in every State shall be bound thereby, any Thing in the Constitution or Laws of any State to the Contrary notwithstanding.

The powers not delegated to the United States by the Constitution, nor prohibited by it to the States, are reserved to the States respectively, or to the people. Powers thereby exercised by the States shall not be commandeered under Laws of the United States.

The Senators and Representatives before mentioned, and the Members of the several State Legislatures, and all executive and judicial Officers, both of the United States and of the several States, shall be bound by Oath or Affirmation, to support this Constitution; but no religious Test shall ever be required as a

Qualification to any Office or public Trust under the United States.

Article VII.

The Ratification of the Conventions of **nine** States, shall be sufficient for the Establishment of this Constitution between the States so ratifying the Same.

Qualification to any Office or public Trust under the United States.

Article VII. Ratification

The Ratification of the Conventions of **thirty-four** States, shall be sufficient for the Establishment of this Constitution between the States so ratifying the Same.

Appendix D: U.S. Representatives

Number of U.S. Representatives By State, Now and Proposed

State	Now	New		State	Now	New
Alabama	7	3		Nebraska	3	1
Alaska	1	1		Nevada	4	2
Arizona	9	4		New Hampshire	2	1
Arkansas	4	2		New Jersey	12	5
California	52	23		New Mexico	3	1
Colorado	8	3		New York	26	12
Connecticut	5	2		North Carolina	14	6
Delaware	1	1		North Dakota	1	1
Florida	28	13		Ohio	15	7
Georgia	14	6		Oklahoma	5	2
Hawaii	2	1		Oregon	6	3
Idaho	2	1		Pennsylvania	17	8
Illinois	17	8		Rhode Island	2	1
Indiana	9	4		South Carolina	7	3
Iowa	4	2		South Dakota	1	1
Kansas	4	2		Tennessee	9	4
Kentucky	6	3		Texas	38	17
Louisiana	6	3		Utah	4	2
Maine	2	1		Vermont	1	1
Maryland	8	4		Virginia	11	5
Massachusetts	9	4		Washington	10	5
Michigan	13	6		West Virginia	2	1
Minnesota	8	3		Wisconsin	8	3
Mississippi	4	2		Wyoming	1	1
Missouri	8	4				
Montana	2	1		**Total**	435	200

Made in the USA
Monee, IL
11 March 2026

45287158R00132